# A Unitarian Perspective

## Rev. Dr. Robert E. Dorris

PublishAmerica
Baltimore

First printing

ISBN: 1-4241-5953-9
PUBLISHED BY PUBLISHAMERICA, LLLP
www.publishamerica.com
Baltimore

Printed in the United States of America

# None May Comprehend

None may comprehend the Mighty One's strength.

Sing hymns of praise to the Lord of Power and Might.
Magnify the One who has daring might.

The One God is the one who hears your prayer and your song.
He is the maker and master of the heavens and the earth.

Be bold with your songs.
Be bold with your praise.

He has given you a resolute mind with independent sway.

All strength and glory is His.
The Holy Spirit is by Him bestowed.

He has given us a tongue which is sharper than a two-edged sword.
None can overcome its might.

Who of us shall have the power and conviction to stay firm and be eager, soul led to do what God has assigned?

Who will this day do what we should have done since the days of old?

The Lord God is ever ready to assist His sons and daughters.
He helps all who are progressing on the Way.

An ever-present Lord is He.
He is the King of the mighty folks.
He is a Father to those who offer their love freely and promote the Law of the Most High.

From Him flows the Holy Spirit to be our guide.
He welcomes our prayer and our hymns of praise.

His power is matchless.
Matchless is His wisdom.

He will be with us in our work.
He will be with all who accept the Holy Spirit to be their aid.
He is the Giver of all that is good.
He will increase us in our power as we grow in the knowledge and wisdom, which He bestows.

He will ever be with those who demonstrate their love.
He will satisfy their longing and fix their mind with the bestowal of the Holy Spirit to aid in all they do.

Without Him we stand in darkness, and the Spirit is concealed.
Without Him many obstructions remain in our way.

Turn to Him.
He will preserve you.
He will guide you and give you increasing bliss.
He will save you from your foolishness and give you great sway.

# Neither the Heavens nor the Earth

Neither the heavens nor the earth can match the greatness of the Lord our God.
Awesome and very mighty is He.

Some like a mighty ocean into which all rivers flow might compare Him to be.
Some may compare Him to a mighty warrior of old.
Some may see Him to be a mighty Spirit.

Greater than all is He.

Over all kinds of greatness, over all kinds of great manly power, He holds sway.
Even greater than the power that brings mountains down, is He.
He is the strong One of every noble deed.
He is the God above all the gods we may conceive.

Matchless is He, to which nothing can compare.

He is our Friend to be desired with all our might.
He only is to be praised by worshipers.
He shows forth His own Holy Spirit to men He calls His own.
He sends forth His auspicious voice and His word.

He stands ready with His mighty strength to aid all of mankind.
He asks only that we take the first step in our return to Him.
He asks that men have faith in the One, the resplendent One.

He makes the lights of heaven to shine forth secure.
He bids the exceedingly wise of mankind to be His worshipers.
On them and them alone will He bestow His Spirit through which flows His aid.

To those who seek their own glory, to those who think that strength on earth is theirs alone, He, with great might, will bring them down.

Be a receiver of the Holy Spirit.
Let your heart be inclined to Him alone.
Let all you do be done in love.
Become most skilled in the Way of the One.
Let none lead you astray.

Our hands cannot contain all the treasures He bestows.
He who accepts God's love never fails.
The Mighty One becomes our unstoppable might.
With the One abide many powers, which become ours to use when we become His ministering Priests.

# Accept the Holy Spirit

Accept the Holy Spirit and be strengthened for great deeds.
Be eager to be of service to the One.

To the Loving ones, the Holy Spirit is quickly given.
To the Loving ones, the Lord of Power, the Holy Synod's might, comes with speed.
To His Loving ones, He gives guidance to meet their needs.

Unfettered are they from the bonds of ignorance.
Shining ones they become.
Victorious always, so great is He.
Unstained by the dust of our former foolishness, He makes us to be.
Into the darkness of man's ignorance He makes us to be shining lights for all to see.

To the little strength we have received from the earth, He adds the mighty strength of His Spirit so we may be of help to all who would like to see.
With joy and happiness He guides our life for all who will perceive.

Those who would change the inhabitants of the earth must take hold of the hand of the One.

They must hold tight to the upholder of heaven and earth.
They must be changed through and through by the Holy Spirit and do all they do in love of God, and love of their fellow man.

Grasp this teaching firmly and do not deviate.

You have now within your power the ability to bring the dead to eternal life.

All you need is at hand if you but understand and believe.

# To Him, the One

To Him, the One, Our Father, I bring my prayer, my hymn, and my praise.
It is He who spreads His bounty about so that all may live.
He gives strength and matchless bounty to all who will receive.

This entire world was designed for worship of the One.
All who come here are to learn their relationship to the One.
He raises those who learn of His Love to a level above the rest.
They are used as Priests and Guides and Teachers to those who come after
them.

Bring your gifts with reverence to the One, and with all your love
Be recreated by His Holy Light, and receive His Holy Power.
For this you were created.

Many praise the One God.
To those who place their trust in Him He gives His help; He aids those who
draw near.
He is the Lover in our praise; none else is worthy of our praise.
As the earth loves all her creatures, so our Father more greatly loves those
who draw near.

Great is the power of the One, the Most High God.
We are His children.
Worthy is He of our love.
He fulfills the wishes of His worshipers, His Children.
All the earth, all the heavens, and all that He has created owes its existence to
Him alone.

He has given to His own, for all time, all victorious might.

# The One God Has Hidden

The One God has hidden for us a goodly treasure to be found.
He has appointed for us His most Holy Priests to be our guides.
We will receive His treasure as a gift when we seek and find the Holy Way.

He will bestow upon us a Sacred Life.
He will be our good Protector.
He will make us a Child of two births as we proceed on the Way.

The One is our Ordainer.

He is the ruler of both gods and men.
He is the One God we yearn for and worship.
He is the Lord of our House and has appointed us as Priests.

May He accept our fair, heart-born praise.
May He guide our words and our actions so that we proceed in the proper way.
His words and teachings are like sweet honey to nourish us each day.

He has desired only good for mankind.
He has placed among men His Choice-worthy Priests.
He has been our Friend, the Lord of our House, and our Protector.

We have repaid Him by turning from the Way.

With our hymns we have extolled Him but we follow not the teachings, which He has given to guide us.

Still He is our Guardian waiting for us to return to the Way.

# To the Lord God

To the Lord God Most High I bring my song of praise and my prayer.
May my thought of Him be resistless.
May He grant my prayer.

To the God Most High who is the Lord of old I dedicate my heart, my mind, my spirit, and my soul.

The words I speak will magnify Him.
To Him will be my words of praise.
To Him will be my prayer.
I will pray to our Father, the Lord, the Most Bounteous Giver.

He gladly hears our praise.
He is the All-moving One, the Wise.
He is the One Lord over all.

I will do all I can to please the Most High God.
I will do all I can with Love.
I will give reverence to all the instructions of God.

The One God is the Vast, the Mighty, and the Wise.

The Most High God has removed my ignorance.
He has put an end to my foolishness.

To Him, our Father, the Most High, I give my praise.
He does encompass the heaven and the earth.
His greatness cannot be exceeded.

In truth, His magnitude surpasses all that we can conceive.
This is the Lord, the God Most High, worshiped by all men.

Through His own strength He has created all that is.
He is the maker and sustainer of all.
With His heart inclined to man, He encompasses us on all sides.

He favors those who worship Him.
He guides and aids them in all that they undertake to do.

He moves swiftly to our aid.

He protects us from those who would lead us astray.
Yes, He who made the mountains and the sea is our strength, our protector,
and our Friend.

It is He who rules alone over all and guards His elect.
Unto Him is our praise and service due.
The God Most High provides His Holy Spirit to the race of men.
He provides it to be our helper and a guide.

To the God Most High the spirit takes our prayer.
Those most pleasing to Him are made in love and service to better mankind.
He knows our every thought and those that come from an undivided heart and
mind.
To these He comes swiftly in answer to our prayer.

# Like the First Instructors

Like the first instructors of mankind we ponder the One who loves our song.
We ponder the Mighty One.
Let us sing of His glory, His far-famed glory.
He is the One who must be praised.

To Him we bring our love and adoration.
It is He who we seek to know well.

The first instructors told us that He desires our Love, our songs, and our praise.

He is the One who created the heavens and the earth.

He is the dispeller of our darkness.
He has established the earth and firmly fixed all the regions.

This is a deed most worthy of all honor.
He is the Wonder Worker.

He forever united the ancient pair, the spirit and the earth.
He is the doer of Marvels.

Each day His marvels are still born afresh.
Each in the proper manner comes forth.
In alternation we become the pair.
'Round heaven and earth from ancient times we have traveled.

Through our travels we become rich in good actions, skilled in our operations.
We become the Sons and Daughters of the One so that we might maintain His perfect friendship.

All our paths, from oldest times, are connected.
We at times rest uninjured, to prepare to renew our journey.
The One with great might preserves the immortal way.
There are many thousand Holy Works that wait to be accomplished.

Many ancient thoughts seek expression.
They wait on the expressions of our love to the God Most High.
The Lord God Most High waits for us to develop and grow in the proper way.
When we are ready and when we are prepared His wondrous thoughts will find expression.

He is a Strong God.
Nothing that He has established from the days of old has perished or been wasted.
Each has had its proper place and purpose to perform.

Splendid is the One and exceedingly Wise.
He is unbending in His purpose.
He has strengthened us with His might.
He leads us day by day and step by step to develop.

The Mighty One has fashioned us to be His Sons and His Daughters too.

He is eternal, the One who was here in the beginning and will be here in the end.

He is a sure leader.

He is our Sire, our Father.

He sets us all upon our course.
He enriches us as we come to Him in prayer.

# Are You a Mighty One?

Are you a mighty one?
Has the One God endowed you with power?
Do those who are in error fear you when you come near?
Do those who are in error fear you when you begin to teach?
Do they shake at your mere presence?

You are within the arms of the Holy One when you have developed and
become His Child.
He is present with you in all that you do.
Many will fear your words and your teachings as a result of their ignorance.

Will you be faithful?
Will you be with those who defy the teachings of the Most High?
If you are faithful, the One Most High will always be at your side.

As a dear Friend and Father you will find the Lord Most High.
He will give you the strength you need to accomplish your task.
He will provide the knowledge and the wisdom too.
You will become a great soul with an easy demeanor.
He will be with you in all you think, do, and say.

In all that you do you will not be harmed.
The Great One is your guide and your protector.
Even in anger, the strongest mortal man will not be able to do you harm.

Many men and women invoke the aid of the One but they do not know who
He is.
They have turned their back to Him so He withholds His aid from them.
When He grants His aid to you, you become a Godlike one to those who have
not received His aid.
You become a worker of mighty deeds.

Easy is His aid to receive.
You must come to the One God with an undivided mind and a loving heart.
Then He will see to your need.

The One God, the God Most High, is ever with us.
It is He who maintains and establishes us.
He bestows upon those who will accept His Holy Spirit to flow through them forever.

Prayers made by the ancient teachers and sages were all addressed to the One.
They prayed for His knowledge and wisdom to be their aid.
May we be enriched by such prayers.

# We Ask God to Bring

We ask God to bring His pure gift to man.
We ask for the gift of knowledge and wisdom.
May we, with wisdom, prepare our minds and prepare our bodies to have the
power to perform the Sacred Rite.

The One brings them to birth, these divine gifts, when we are free from spot
and stain.
The Holy Spirit purifies us when we return to the One.

These gifts being received, the recipients never grow old.
All beings will tremble at their mighty strength.
They become the very strongest, both of heaven and earth.

The Children of God are a beauty to behold.
Through them the very spirit of God shines forth.
The radiance of the love they have shows forth for all to see.

The Spirit of God is their power and strength.
They fill their portion of the world with teachings of the One.
They are ever wandering around the whole earth.

They demonstrate the love of the Sacred Rite.
They are always endeavoring to lead those in darkness to the never failing
spring.
The water of life they offer to all to drink.

They will guide us swiftly on the Way.
They ask us to receive the Holy Spirit as our strength.
Mighty do we become with this wondrous power.
Brilliant do we become when the Holy Spirit is within us.

Exceedingly wise are they who possess the Holy Spirit.
They become lights that shine into the darkness of mankind's ignorance, which all may see.
As Children of God they become His High Priests.
Through their might, their love, all will come closer to the truths of God.

They remain with man as a friend.
In them you see the Spirit and the Earth united and working in harmony.
Many will see them as beings filled with light.

The Children of God dwell in the House of Wealth.
Their wealth is the knowledge and wisdom that comes from God.
They are endowed with mighty vigor and infinite power, which aids them in completing all their tasks.

Many will think them wanderers from the way.
They are self-moving and never weary.
They will teach and speak in ways that are contrary to what many consider to be firm.
With their bright spirits and new views they will make the many to reel.

The Children of God will invoke Him with prayer.
They will be worshipers of the One.
They will cleave for happiness to the truth of the One.
Many will think them impetuous wanderers, far from the way.

In truth, their help is God.
In truth, they are guarded by God.
He verily is their strength, which surpasses that of all mankind.
They are ever honorable and their teachings will prosper all who will follow the Way.

They, worshipers of the One, are given glorious strength.
They are invincible and carry with them the wisdom and knowledge of God.
They teach what is praiseworthy and to be known to all men.
May we listen to what these Sons and Daughters of God teach.

May we be enriched by their prayers.

May we, too, become the Sons and Daughters of the One God and bring enrichment to the lives of mankind.

# Be One Minded

Be One minded and wise.
Worship the One God.
Bring your prayers and cares to Him.
In all you think, say, or do, draw nigh to the Holy One.

The One God is approached by the way of the Holy Law.
The Holy Law controls all life in the heavens and the earth.
We are like the growing baby, learning as we proceed on the Way.

Be grateful that this is so.
We are ever learning about our dwelling place.
We are ever learning how to be more fruitful.
We are ever learning to become a wholesome stream.
None can check our course.

We are all kin, brothers and sisters.
We are each learning to complete our journey in our separate ways.
Wherever we go and whatever we are led to do, the One God is our guide.

He places wisdom in our minds when we wake from our sleep of ignorance.
When He bestows the Holy Spirit we become Sages of His Holy Law.
We continue to grow like some young creature till we become true Children
of the One and return to our home.

# Be Like a Ray

Be like a ray of the God Most High.
Be like a dispenser of wealth.
Be like the life breath, which is our life.
Be like the Holy One's own son or daughter.

The One God gives us safety and gives us a pleasant home.
The One God gives us fame among the common folk.
The One God gives us to be everyone's friend.
The One God gives us the power to do all that needs to be done.

With the Holy Spirit He inflames us.
With the Holy Spirit He cares for us.
With the Holy Spirit He shines forth through us.
With the Holy Spirit He prepares the way for us.

To those who are in darkness He seems to strike with terror.
To those who are in darkness He seems to be a flame.

He is the Master of the Present.
He is the Master of the future life.
He is our Lover and our Lord.

To Him lead all our ways.
To Him we attain when we pray.
To Him we return.
To Him who is our Father and our Friend we will go.

# The One God

The One God is our Father and our Friend.
Ever He claims obedience as a King.
He is gracious in giving us peace.
He blesses us with mental power.
He fills us full of thought.
Great Priests He would have us to be.

In His hand He bears all manly might.
Those who are ignorant He strikes with fear.
Those who are filled with understanding find Him where they are.
They are with Him when they have formed prayers within their heart.

He is the unborn who holds the broad earth up.
With His words He has created the heavens, the earth, and the sky.
With His love He guards the home of man.
With His love He has given life to all.
With His love He goes from home to home.

Whoever has known Him has welcomed Him into their home.
Whoever has known Him has approached the originator of all the Holy Law.
To those who welcome Him He bestows great wealth.
Those who welcome Him release His love and perform the Sacred Rite.

It is He who aids us to grow.
It is He who guides us to be fruitful.
It is He who is the Wise.
It is He who is life to all men.
It is He who the Sages honor.

# God Is Commingled

God is commingled in all that we know.
God is active in unveiling us from night.
God is with all that stands or moves.
The One God is the sole God preeminent above all.

All men may be joyful in His power.
From this living One we are born.
All men truly share in the One God while they keep, in their accustomed ways, His eternal law.

The thought of law is strong.
All strive to know the law.
All works that we perform in our striving, He quickens them all.
Whoever brings their love and their gifts to Him He will vouchsafe the wealth of knowledge and wisdom.

He will make us as Priests to all of mankind because He alone is Lord.
Men yearn to become His Children and are not disappointed in their hope.

To those who eagerly hear His word, He fulfills their wish.
They become His Children and obey their Father's instruction.
He opens to them the many doors to His wealth.
He is their Friend and Lord of their house.

# Like a Lover

Like a lover, the One God has filled and joined the two worlds, the world of Spirit and the world of man.

When born we are encompassed by them both.
The One God is Father of the gods, and yet we are His Children.
He is our Father too.

It is the humble and the Sage who will discern this.
God is the bliss giver who must be drawn to man.
Still He sits in the middle of our house waiting for us to acknowledge Him.

In Him we are born.
He is our dwelling place.
He bears with us, as we become common folk.
He waits on us till he can say, "This is my Child in whom I am well pleased.
What a time men have until they call, when they return, I grant again to them their god-like power."

None can break the Holy Laws.
All must return to be granted audience.
None can come by boasting.
None can come by taking advantage of their peers.
None may come by living a life of disgrace.

All may come by remembering me.
All may come by striving to live a sacred life.
All may come in love, with an undivided heart and mind.

To those who come in any humble way bearing themselves in love to God will find unbarred all the doors.

They may all return to their fair place.
They may return to their Father's home.

# May We Live

May we live as pious men.
May we come to God in prayer.
May the Spirit of God pervade each of our acts.
May the One God, the Maintainer, Establisher, and Observer of the Holy
Laws always look favorably upon the race of mortal man.

The One is the creator of the waters.
The One is the creator of the woods.
The One is the creator of all things that do not move.
The One is the creator of all things that do move.
He is in the rock, and He is in the house.
He is the Immortal One.
Regardless of what we may think, He cares for all mankind.

The One is a Lord of richness to those who demonstrate their love.
He is with all who strive to live the Sacred Life.
He protects these beings that come to Him with careful thought.
He knows full well the races of both the gods and men.

He is the One God of all.
We may not all worship alike, but it is the One who makes us strong.
He knows all who strive to understand His law.
He knows all that move and stand.
When He has been won and accepts our way He makes effectual all our Holy
works.
He aids us on our way.

He sets our values and brings us to the light of knowledge and wisdom.
Men have learned to serve Him in many and sundry ways.
In all ages and at all times, He is with those who truly seek the way.

# When We Love

When we love the loving One, the One God, He urges us forward.
He urges us to break through our limiting views.
He urges us to leave behind the darkness of our ignorance.

Our Father has set before us all that is firm.
He has made for us a way to reach even the highest heaven.
He has founded for us the light of day.

The loving One has established all in order.
He has made our service performed with love fruitful.
He is our longing faithful Friend.
With His aid we become most active.
He feeds us with the teachings of the Wise.
He provides us with strength.

When we welcome Him into our house, He causes it to grow bright and noble.
He becomes our companion in all that we think, say, or do.

When man accepts the Holy Spirit, our mighty Father is pleased.
He knows what we have done and will do.
He frees us from our imprisonment.
God bestows His splendor upon His sons and daughters.

Whosoever has invited the Spirit of God within their dwelling receives His blessing day to day.

They bring their prayer and worship to God and receive His love each day.
God will double their substance and provide to them knowledge and wisdom.

All who strive to lead a sacred life wait on and serve the God Most High.
He knows all who truly strive to journey on the Way.
He provides His loving care to all who seek to know Him.

When men are filled with the light of the Spirit of God, He prepares them for increased responsibility.

He provides them with the straight path to walk within.
Those who walk the path, He holds blameless and well provides for their needs.

He provides them with God-like thoughts and swiftly guides them in the way.
Never are they alone, for the Lord God is ever present.
He is their protector and their guide.

The Lord our God will not break the ancestral Friendship He established of old with mankind.

He will continue to endow His Sages with the deepest knowledge.
Never since the ages of old has He left mankind without His guides.
Never has He allowed those of mankind who worship Him to be without His protection and His aid.

# The One Is Holding

The One is holding many gifts for men and women.
The gifts of His Higher Powers would humble even those who think themselves wise.
He is forever granting all immortal bounties.

Even today the One is bestowing His gifts.

Many who think themselves infallible and wise have searched for the One and have not found Him.

Only those who come like a babe, a child, will find the One who is still around and about us.

Many have become worn and weary trying to find the path of the One.
Only when they come as children, will they discover and reach the home of the One.

The most noble have all come to the One in this way.
Even if they have only served the One for three years, they have won for themselves Holy names.

These individuals should receive our honor because they have become nobly born and they have dignified their bodies.

We should make them known to all upon the earth.
These noble ones have revealed to the world the powers and teachings of the One.
Discerning at a distance, this mortal band has demonstrated God's love to those in every station of life.

They have taught that God will come to meet with men and women wherever they are.

High or low, Rich or poor, in Sickness or in Health, God may be found wherever you are.

Everyone may draw nigh to the One by one approach.
All become one-minded as a child.
All will gather before the One in loving worship.
The One becomes their Father and Friend.
His eye is always upon them for their protection.
They make use even of their bodies to be of service to the One.

The noble-born soon discover the mystic things.
They may even appear to be Holy Ones to a normal mortal man.
Yet, primarily they have discovered that the One is within all things and within each individual.

With these discoveries they become One-minded.
They preserve the Way of the One.

They know the One is the eternal guardian of all.
They know the One is the knower of man's works.
They know the One has provided for us what is good.
They know the One maintains a constant course.
They know the One provides for our subsistence.

They endeavor to become deeply skilled and knowledgeable of all the paths established by the One.

They become an envoy for the One, offering their love and services to all who would draw near.

They become knowers of the Law.
They know the pathways from heaven.
They become full of good thoughts.

They are able to discern the ways that open the prison doors established by mankind in its foolishness.

They know that the race of mankind is still supported by the One despite our ignorance.

They may guide all noble operations.
They may guide in setting up for an individual a path that leads to life immortal.
They may guide individuals to discern when they have the Holy Spirit's support.
They may even guide us to discern the powers of our Mother, the earth.

When the Immortal God, the One, made our eyes, He gave us a gift most beautiful and glorious.

He gave us a way of observing and recognizing the workings of the One that we might live in a harmonious way.

# The One Is Like

The One is like a Father providing us with sustenance.
The One is like a Wise Man who guides those who will follow His instructions.
The One is like a Guest, for He loves pleasant lodging.
The One is like a Priest, for He prospers His servants' dwelling.

The One is like a Savior, because He protects all who are true minded.
With His power He protects all those who perform good acts.
He is the Truthful One, glorified by many.
He is our very life-breath that gives us joy.
All must strive to win Him.

He is the all-sustaining God.
He dwells on the earth like a king surrounded by faithful friends.
All those who accept and dwell in His presence will sit in safety.

The One God makes our settlements secure.
Each individual who chooses to serve Him will find Him always in his or her dwelling.

Those who serve Him receive splendor in abundance.
They become dear to all men who are seeking to learn about the wisdom and knowledge of the One.

Those who worship the One receive the bestowal of a full life filled with love.
So abundant is the love they have, they seek always to share.

They share the knowledge and wisdom they have received which will flow through them like an abundant stream.

Soliciting the favor of the One, they will become dispensers of the Holy Law. They will be able to see how all paths flow together.

Soliciting the favor of the One, they become like Holy Ones who have gained glory in heaven.

They will be able to see how all things work in harmony.

May we and all who worship the One be led by wisdom and knowledge.
May we learn in abundance so that we may serve as guides of the One.
May we learn to teach and explain how the One has filled the heavens and the earth.
May we learn to teach and explain how the One encompasses the whole world like a shadow.

Aided by the One may we learn to discern the truth and have the ability to explain it, man to man.

Aided by the One may we learn to teach all men how to live in harmony.
May we become Lords of the wealth of knowledge transmitted to us through our ancestors and our Father.

May the One accept our hymns of praise.
May He be our Ordainer and fill us with a pleasant and loving heart and spirit.
May we have the power to use, in an appropriate way, the many God-sent gifts that we have received.

May we have the power to live in the Sacred Way.

# As We Go Forth

As we go forth to lead a Sacred life, it is the One God who hears what we say. Even if we think He is far away He hears our words and He responds to what we say.

It is the One who has from the most ancient of days preserved mankind from the carnage of our ways.

When people are gathered together it is He who is present to see and hear what they do and say.

It is He who has preserved for His household those who worship Him with their love.

Let men say what they may.

It is the One who gives to all from His wealth.
He shares His knowledge with all who are seeking the way.

It is He who maintains every house and guides those seeking the way.
It is He who provides an envoy to those who love and want to learn of the way.
It is He who strengthens those who wish to lead a Sacred Life.

The One provides the means for all to become sons and daughters of strength. All men and women who seek happiness in their God may share in His strength.
All who come to the One with their love will receive His aid to lead a Sacred Life.

This fair and shining One accepts all thoughts we have when we are motivated by love.

He will guide each of us in a way that we can understand.

He will embrace us as we are and where we are.
He will guide us with His Love to walk in a Sacred Way.

He will lead us step by step.
He will protect us all from harm.
Ever forward will we progress with the One to aid us.
Stronger and stronger we will become when we remain with Him in a Loving Way.

This is a gift we receive from Him—To live always in love as we travel the Sacred Way.

# May God Be Delighted

May God be delighted in my hymn.
May God be delighted with the words that I speak.

Now to the Wise One we will say,
Accept and find precious our much availing prayer.

Who, O Lord, of men do you consider your kin?
Who of men do you consider a worthy worshiper?
On whom is mankind ever dependent?
Who are you, O Lord, that we should worship you?

Are you not the kinsman of all mankind?
Are you not mankind's well-beloved Friend?
Are you not a Friend to whom all Friends may bring their cares?

Bring us to the proper understanding.
Bring to us the knowledge required to lead a Sacred Life.
Bring to us the wisdom to proceed in the proper way.
Bring us to the Way, the Pathway to return home.

# How May the Mind

How may the mind draw nigh to the One?
What may we do in our life to please Him?
What hymns may we sing to bring us His blessing?
How can we gain His power to lead a sacred life?
What can we do to ensure we will obtain His love?

Come close.
Sit down as if you were a child.
Listen.
Let no one be a deceiver to you.
Let no one lead you astray.
Seek for one to be your leader who loves the One and who loves mankind as
if they were his own.

May heaven and earth bear witness to these words.

The all-pervading One has love for all.
The worship of many gods does not gain for us favor.
To make numerous sacrifices does not ward off curses.

The One God is glad to welcome all who give Him their love.
To these and these alone will He bestow from His Spirit.
The One is a bounteous giver to all who demonstrate their love of God and
their love of mankind.

The Priests who with their voice and with their life demonstrate the Love of
God and the Love of mankind deserve our honor and praise.

To them we may bring our children to learn of the One.
Theirs is the task of gleaning the truth from a multitude of teachings.

Theirs is the task of presenting to us the best that they are capable of understanding.

Theirs is the task of awakening us to the Sacred Way.

Theirs is the task of guiding us to the One, to guide us so that we may find our way home.

Such a Sage may be considered a Sage of Sages.

With Love they will worship the One.

With Love they will guide mankind.

Our task now is to truthfully worship the One.

Our task now is to demonstrate the joy in our life that comes from knowing Him.

Our task now is to demonstrate our love of mankind.

# How Shall We Show

How shall we show our love of the One?
What can we say?
What can we do?

How can we become His heralds to mankind?
How can we demonstrate to our best the Way?
How can we acknowledge that the One, who is deathless, ever true to His
Own Law, resides in the midst of mankind?

Come forward, those of you who wish to be His heralds.
Come forward and bring to Him your love.
Come forward and do your best to lead a Sacred Life.

When you come forward to serve your God, He knows you full well.
He knows all who would worship Him in Truth and in Spirit.
He knows all who seek for God with Body, Mind, and Spirit.
He knows who are pretenders, too.

You see, the One is our mental power.
He is within all men and women.
He is the One who prompts us to desire a perfect life.
He is the One who brings us to strive for all that is good.
He is the One who is like a friend who would have us experience all that is
wondrous.

It is He who leads all who would be pious.
It is He who accomplishes all that is marvelous.

May the One accept our love.
May He accept with love our hymns and our devotion.

May He grant us His strength, His knowledge, and His wisdom.
May He stir our thoughts with vigor.
May He guide us on the Sacred Way.

The One is ever true to His established order.
He is the One who has been praised in all ages.

To those who observe His Ways, He will come with love and splendor.

# The One Is Swift

The One is swift and keen to aid those who would be teachers of the Holy Law.
The One is swift and keen to aid those who would glorify Him by following in the Sacred Way.

The One will meet us where we are when we turn to Him.
The One will meet us as we are when we turn to Him.
He will meet with all who worship Him by bringing to Him their love.

We are to do our best to demonstrate God's glory.
We are to do our best to set an example to others of how to live in the Way.
We are to do our best to make proper use of the talents and knowledge we have been given.

When we do our best, the One is glorified.
When we do our best, obstacles are overcome.
When we do our best, Love will encompass us.

It is most pleasant when the Sons and Daughters of the One do their best.
He will be with them in their song.
He will be with them when they pray.
He will be with them in all they think, do, or say.

# The Holy One Knows

The Holy One knows our beginnings.
He knows who strives to be honorable.
He knows who strives to be true.
He knows who strives to be active workers.

He knows full well the manner in which we lead our life.
His Spirit is all around and within us.
He knows whom to bless.
He knows who will smile when He comes to their aid.
He knows those who detest the Way.

He will come to us with the level of instruction we need in our form of
worship.
He will guide us to the most direct paths of Order.
He will fill us full to our capacity to comprehend.

The One is the bestower of knowledge and wisdom.
He will make us Sons and Daughters of Strength.
He will fill us to our capacity and keep us safe.

He, the One, is kind, good, and wise.
He is the One we exalt with our living and our song.
He is the One who appears to us in many forms.
He is the One who will shine His blessings on us.

He will be with us in our day.
He will be with us in our night.
He waits for us to ask Him to be our guide.

We ask Him to give approval to all our rites.
We ask Him to give us favor.

We ask Him to give us His aid.
We ask Him to encompass us with His Love.

We ask Him to give us increase in our knowledge and wisdom.
We ask Him to make us worthy with our choices.
Most of all we ask Him to make us invincible.

We ask Him to give and give.
We forget that it is through His grace alone that we have the knowledge and wisdom to lead our life.

We forget that it is He who through His grace supports all our life.
It is through His grace that we receive His favor that we may live.

We are told to compose our hymns and our prayers with care.
We are told to watch our thoughts and our words.
We are told to do all we do with love for God and love for mankind.

When we do all in love we will not fail or fall.
God will be with us and increase and prosper us.

When we forget this rule, we are on our own.
When we turn our backs on Him, He will turn from us.
Such is His Rule.

Keen and swift is He.

Let us not forget to give Him our praise and our love.
This is all He has ever asked from His Children in order to receive His aid and His Love.

# When We Receive

When we receive the Holy Spirit we are overcome with joy.
We are ever thankful that our ignorance and foolishness have been driven away.
We give thanks and praise to God, for He holds us in His own sway.

The flowing Holy Spirit gladdens us.
It becomes our strength and aids us to travel the royal way.

We are given courage to go forward.
We are given courage to be bold.
The One becomes our might and guides us on our way.

The Life-fostering Spirit becomes our Host.
It protects us and guides us.
It guides our every step on the Way.

With the receipt of the Holy Spirit comes great responsibility.
We leave behind wrathfulness.
We turn our backs on our former ways.
We are no longer free to travel in ignorant ways.
We are to travel with the One upon the Royal Way.

We are to rejoice in the spirit that is our guide.
We are to seek prosperity for our friends.
We are to bring our friends to the Way.

To the One alone belongs unconquered might.
To Him we have committed our way.
He is the rock upon which we stand.
In His hands is the Way.

In His arms is our strength and might.
To Him alone we look for guidance and aid.

To Him alone is due our praise.
To Him alone do we raise our prayer.
To Him alone do we give thanks upon the Royal Way.

Mighty is His power—We know of no stronger might.
He holds all in His sway.

All the worlds would tremble in terror at His wrath, but He and His love hold
firm to those who are dear.
All would shake out of fear if they were to know His full power.
None could stand against Him if that were His way.

In His might He has set firm the heavens and the earth.
In His love he has established and maintained mankind.
Such is His Royal Way.

He has not wanted our fear but our love.
Such is His Royal Way.

There is not, in our knowledge, any who pass the One in His strength or His
love.
In Him is our manliness, our insight, power, and might.
In Him is our very existence.

Still as in days of old, whatever rite of worship is performed, He is the One
God and Lord of All.
However mankind may make their prayer and their praise, all are united, and
in the One they meet.
Such is His Royal Way.

# Mankind Has Developed

Mankind has developed many views concerning God.
To some He is a Slayer.
To some He is the Giver of joy and strength.
To some He is a mighty Warrior.
To some He simply does not exist.
But what is He to you?

We call upon Him whenever we are in trouble.
We call upon Him for every problem whether it be great or small.
We call upon Him to be our aid in deeds of might.
We call upon Him to bring us abundance and wealth.
We call upon Him to strengthen even the feeble.
We call upon Him to give us an easy life.
We call upon Him to lead us into the Sacred Way.

He is mighty in His wisdom.
He is terrible to those who have forsaken the Way.
He is strong beyond compare.
He is the bountiful giver to those who travel the Way.

He filled the earth and created its atmosphere so that we could live.
He established and maintains all the lights in the heavens.
He provided for man's sustaining food.
He provided for us ways to share in His bounties and power.

None like the One have ever been born.
None who are born will be like Him for us to compare.
He is the One who is above and within us all.

May the One continue to lend us His aid.
May the One continue to share His bounties with us.

May the One continue to be righteous-hearted.
May the One continue to gather and protect us with His hands.
May the One continue to provide us with His love.

May we be found worthy of His continued support.
May we continue to share with Him our love.
May we continue to grow and develop so that we may properly be called "The Children of the Way."

He has provided to man the ability to choose.
He will be to us as a friend.
He will be to us as a father.
He will be to us as our hearts desire.

Are we worthy?
Are we willing to choose the proper way?
Are we ready to discover the Lord, the One?
Which will we choose; His Love or His Wrath?

Before you, have been laid the paths of Life and those of death.
It is for you alone to choose.

# Graciously Listen

Graciously listen to our words and our song.
Be not negligent in learning about the Way.
As the One has filled us with joy, we seek to share that joy with all who care
to listen.
The yoke we accept from the One is to us a joy indeed.

Many are His friends who have risen and passed beyond this mortal life.
Many Sages have praised Him and instructed us about the Way.
Now the One offers His yoke to all who would obtain His knowledge and
wisdom.
Indeed it is a joy to bear.

We will reverence the One who is so fair.
We will reverence the One who encircles us with love.
It is our wish to be with Him always, to accept the yoke of His love.

He will, in truth, be with all who accept His love and travel on the Holy Way.
He will be with all who truly wish to know the Way.
He will be with all who think in a pious and loving way.
He will be with all who accept the yoke of the Sacred Way.

The One is the Lord of a hundred powers.
He controls the extremes of powers, both the right and the left.
He guides us to maintain the middle way.
With His Holy Spirit He draws near to all who would travel in the middle
way.
All who will accept the yoke of love will be filled to the brim.

With my prayer, I ask that I may be found worthy.
May I be found worthy to receive the yoke of love.

May I be found worthy to be filled with the Holy Spirit.
May the One forever hold me in His hands
May I be found worthy to always be an ambassador of the Way.

# The One Protects

The One protects and guards mortal man.
He provides His aid by giving us knowledge and wisdom.
He provides His aid by filling us with the Holy Spirit to be our guide.

The One gives us to partake of His bowl.
He will conduct the pious to the Sacred Way.
He will take delight in our prayers motivated by love.

He will bestow His blessing on those who truly seek to serve mankind and their God.
He will dwell with them and they with Him.
He will teach them of His Law.
Those who travel on the sacred way will receive the outpouring of His gifts.

Those who endeavor to do good deeds and to live in the sacred way will receive vital power.

Those who would hoard the knowledge and wealth will be stripped of the power and wealth they had previously received.

Forever are we to walk the paths of Sacred Love.
Forever are we to be guardians of the Law.
Forever are we to live in a way worthy of our deathless birth.

When we have received the Holy Spirit to aid in our auspicious work, it makes us aware of its voice.

We will know in truth that the One finds delight in us.
He truly delights when we draw near.

# The Holy Spirit Has Been Prepared

The Holy Spirit has been prepared for you by the One, the God Most High.
Come to Him and become a mighty one, a bold one of the Way.
May the Spirit fill you full with vigor as the Sun fills the air with its rays.

Bring your life to the One of irresistible might.
He will guide you to the Sacred Way.
He will accept your words, your prayers, and your praise.
He will guide you in the Sacred Works that are to be performed by man.

He will take away your ignorant and foolish ways.
You will receive the yoke of love in answer to your prayer.
The voice of the Holy Spirit will be made known to you and forever onward
it will be your guide.

You will receive from the One the cloak of immortality.
You will be gladdened to follow in His most excellent Way.
The constant stream of the Holy Spirit will flow to you and through you when
you take a seat with the One and accept the yoke of the Holy Law of Love.

Give glory now to the One with your words and your song.
Speak of Him in your solemn eulogies.
To receive His Spirit will make you glad.
To bestow the Spirit upon you will make Him glad too.
Pay due reverence to the might of His Love Supreme.

There is no better guide than the One.
Accept His yoke of Love.
He will guide you to perform many good deeds, which may be undone by
none.

He alone bestows on mortal man the gifts that come from His Love.
He is a ruler of resistless power.
He is truly the One.

Mankind has no gift worthy enough to present to the One except our undivided love.
Without this love of Him we have no gift, we have no answer to our prayer.
We have no one who will hear our songs of praise.
We have no one who will guide us in our words and deeds.

He has prepared the Holy Spirit for all who are prepared to give Him their undivided love.

He bestows His Spirit to all who are genuine in their love.
They gain thereby tremendous might to do all that they can do.
They who are at the side of the One rejoice.
They forever seek to do good, guided by His love.

Forever will they be in touch with the One who will fill them full to their capacity with the Spirit of Love.
Step by step they will be led to increase their capacity.

With Love they may become exceeding wise.
They will grow in knowledge and wisdom when they follow closely His many laws.
They will grow in their capacity for good.

In His arms they will ever be.
With Him they will be able to guide others to the Sacred Way of Love.

Have you found what you have been seeking for so many years?
Have you found what you have sought?

Have you recognized the essential requirement?
Have you learned the Way of the One?

Will you accept His yoke today?
Will you come today?

Will you come to the One and accept His Spirit?
Will you commit to His service and the service of mankind?

God is present now!
He is near to all of us.
He will bestow His Spirit on all who would be considered His Children.
They become members of His household.
They share in the wealth of His knowledge and wisdom.
They become His people.

Come to Him now.
Come before Him with your heart, your mind, your body, and your soul.
Honor Him with your thoughts, your words, and your deeds.
Worship Him for the right reason.

He will bless you while you are still a mortal person.
He will encompass you with His love.
He will comfort you and be with you when you commit to Him.
Speak your words to the One, and He will take heed of what you say.

He will not let His bounteous gifts be bestowed except to those who come with their love.
He will not let His saving help fail us.

He is the Good.

He is the One we call our Father.

He is ready at any time to encompass us with love.
He will measure out to us all that we are capable of comprehending and receiving.

He is a lover of mankind.

Will you come to Him with your love?

Will you come today?

# The Sons and Daughters

The Sons and Daughters of the One go forth with love guiding their way.
They act swiftly and are doers of mighty deeds.
As the One has made the heavens and the earth to grow; in following the Sacred Way they grow in wisdom and in knowledge.

To the One, His Children are a sheer delight.

The Children of the One grow and develop till they attain perfect strength and greatness.

The One has established their abode with Him in the heaven of their heart.
As His Children, they have put on His glory.
Their words, their prayer, and their songs generate a mighty spirit to accomplish many good deeds.

The Children of the One seem to shine as if surrounded by a golden light.
The Spirit of the One flows through them driving away each adversary from their path.

Those who follow in their paths receive their sense of love, peace, and tranquility.

Mighty warriors will tremble when the Children of the One come near.
Their weapons of war and hate are powerless compared to the strength of the Children of the One.

Most of the conflicts experienced by man could be avoided simply by following the Way of the One.

Sickness, disease, hatred, wars, and death would simply vanish if everyone would follow in the teachings of the paths of the One.

Come forward.
Let your feet bring you forward to the open and loving arms of the One.
Sit in His presence, for a place has been prepared for you.
Delight yourselves in the love, the knowledge, and the wisdom of the One.

Strong as you may be in your mortal strength, it is nothing compared to the strength you will develop as you come forward to become a Child of the One.

With His Holy Spirit flowing through you, you will experience the sheer delight of His Love and His Power.

No longer will you find the need to fight.
No longer will you strive in the conflicts that lead to your wars.
Before you, every ignorant creature will be afraid.
To foolish and wicked men you will be a terror to behold.
These men, even if they are kings, will tremble when you draw near.

When the Spirit of the One is received you will be able to perform many heroic deeds.
The One will teach you how to be most skillful in its use.

When the Spirit of the One is received your voice will become the instrument of your power.

When you send forth your words, even the clouds and the sea will be within your ability to command.

The One is a bountiful giver to those who accept His love and walk in the proper way.
He will give them the power to accomplish many glorious deeds.

To those who come to Him with their love, their open hearts and minds, He will quench their thirst with the water of life.

To those who come to Him with their willingness to be of service to Him and to do good for mankind, He will fill them with the Holy Spirit so that they may be of help to those in need.

They will become His Sages to take His instruction to mankind.
No longer will their words be their own, but the words of the One who has instructed them to bring enlightenment to mankind.

His Children, men or women, who go forth as Sages and Teachers of the Way of the One, The Holy Way, will always be encompassed by His love.

He will shelter them.
He will ensure that no harm comes to them, and they will not die.
Such are His gifts to these noble ones.

# The Best of Guardians

The Best of Guardians is already within each member of mankind.
It has made our inmost being its dwelling place.

Listen to my words.
The One we honor,
The One we worship,
The One to whom we send our prayer,
The One listens to our call.
That One we have within.
He is ever present with each of us.

The Strong One who has brought to you His Sages and Teachers, you have
already within.
In Him you move.
In Him you live.
Such is the One you have been searching for.

You may travel the world.
You may search forever in vain.
You may go from teacher to teacher.
You will never find Him until you look within.

Let all hear these words.
If you want strength that surpasses all men look to the One.
If you want the wisdom and knowledge that is beyond compare.
If you want a Spirit that is brighter than the sun look to the One.
You must look for Him and find Him within.

God's loving help is swift and always available.
But, many of us wait until the autumn of our life before we seek that loving
help that is within.

How fortunate that mortal shall be who in his or her youth begins to search within.

The One will come to you according to your heart's desire.

He will unveil Himself to all who come to Him with their love.

The One is your true strength.

The One will manifest for you true greatness.

The One will remove the veils that keep you in ignorance, but first you must meet Him within.

His light will drive away the darkness of ignorance.

Find the One—The Best Guardian—By looking within.

# Few in Number

Few in number are those who will accept these teachings.
Few in number will be those who display the fullness of the Holy Spirit, the fullness of the One.
These few will never be humbled.
They will always be active and full of strength.
They may seem impetuous to man, but they are the best loved of the One.

Whatever their path may be,
Wherever they are directed to go,
Whatever they undertake to do,
You can be assured it is not them but the One who is guiding them on their way.
It is the One who directs their tasks and gives them the very words they speak.

Many will travel the earth, themselves admirers of their own mightiness.
They will claim to represent the One.
In truth they represent none other than themselves.
They will tire and become weak and worn because they put upon themselves and others the yoke of their own teachings.
They may see themselves as movers and shakers, but the Spirit is not with them to guide their way.
Their ways often lead to greater ignorance.
They are far from the Way.

The few are self-moving.
Despite some of advanced human age, they will seem youthful in their way.
They will hold Lordly sway and be empowered by the Spirit with power and might.
They will be truthful in all they do.
They will follow the blameless Way.

Their Strong Host, the One, will be their Protector.
He will be with them to fulfill each of their prayers.

These few will speak only at the direction of their heavenly Father.
They will seek out and expose ignorance wherever it may be.
They will use the Spirit within to overcome man's foolishness.
Never for their own glory will they teach or act.
Their concern is for the glory of the One and what is good for mankind.

Men may praise the few, but they direct all praise to the One.
They are armed with His words and to His Home will they return.

# Come Forth

Come forth, those of you who claim mighty power.
Come forth with the knowledge and wisdom of the One.
Show to us your mighty power.

Come forth and tell us of God's glory.
Come forth in the brilliance of the Spirit of God.
Come forth with His words, which remove the veil of ignorance.
Come forth with His words, which will end our foolish ways.
Come forth if you dare.

Where is the beauty of your words?
Where are the words that will stir our spirit from its sleep?
For your sake, we hope you are very mighty and wellborn.
Are you able to set the Stone in motion?

Day after day, day after day, nothing seems to change.
Where are the teachings?
Where is the Spirit that will bring the answers to our prayer?
You tell us to be solemn in worship, but where are the answers to our prayer?
Where are the teachers who receive answers to their prayer?
Where are the teachers who can lead us to the well and give us to drink of the
water of life?

If you are able, come forth to us with the teachings of the One.
Share with us the knowledge and wisdom of the One, as you are able.

Bring to us the Spirit you have received from the One.
Bring to us the noble teachings.
Be to us the voice of the One.
Come to us if you dare.

# May the Powers

May the Powers of the One come to us.
May they surround us on every side.
May we never be deceived.
May the One be with us and protect us.
May the One be with us day to day.
May He be unceasing in His care.

May the favor of the One be ours.
May He lead us to live in a righteous way.
The friendship of the One we have devotedly sought.
May He show us the way from death to eternal life.
May He lead us in the Sacred Way.

We call the One with words passed on to us from ancient times.
We seek His friendship, His spirit, and His love.
We seek to establish or know our relationship to Him.

May His Spirit bring to us that pleasant medicine—the ability to know.
May we know of our relationship to our Mother, the earth.
May we know of our relationship to our Father, the establisher of all.
May His Holy Spirit hear and answer our call.

We invoke for aid the One who reigns supreme.
We invoke the Lord of all.
We invoke the Inspirer of the soul.
May He be our guard and guide.
May He do with us what is necessary for our good.

May the One prosper us, for He is the Master of all wealth.
May the One keep us from harm.

The One is with us when we perform the Holy Rite.
The Sages have taught us His Spirit is more brilliant than the sun.
Let the One who is our protection come to us.
May He both keep us from harm and keep us from doing harm to those who come to us for aid.

May the One open our ears so that we will listen to what is good.
May the One open our eyes so that we may see what is good.
May the One make our limbs and bodies firm so that we may attain to do that which is good.

May we properly accomplish that which has been set for this term of our life.
May we be found delightful to Him.

If a hundred years stand before us, and our sons become fathers in turn, separate not from us, we will cry to the One.
Do not leave us or break from us in the midst of our course of this fleeting life.

Let us always remember that the Earth is our Mother, and our Sire is the One, the Lord and Father of all.
We are the children of these two.
All that have been born and all who shall be born should honor these two.

# May We Be Appointed

May we be appointed Sages who will give us the straight guidance.
May we be appointed Teachers who know the One.
May we be appointed Priests who will lead us in accord with the truth, which comes from the One.

They are to lead, guide, and teach us from the wealth of knowledge and wisdom of the One.

They are to guard forevermore the Holy Laws.

May they lead us to the shelter of the One.
May they keep us safe from following on the wrong way.
These Sages, Teachers, and Priests may seem as Immortal Gods to normal mortal men.

They have accepted the unending task to drive away our ignorant and foolish ways.
They will chase these enemies away.

May they mark out our paths.
May they lead us to bliss.
May they lead us to the One who is worthy to be adored.

They have traveled the course and have returned to enrich us with the knowledge and wisdom of the One.

They will be a blessing to those who desire to follow the way.

The Spirit of the One and the waters of life are the foods of the children who keep the Law of the One.

Love we will receive in the night.
Love we will receive in the day.
Love from our Father will encompass us.

May the tree of knowledge be full of good things for us.
May we develop the wisdom to make proper use of its gifts for the glory of our God.

Let it be that our Sages, Teachers, and Priests are gracious to us and bring us up in the proper way.

Let it be that they lead us with kindness to the Holy Way, the Love of the One.

# The Holy Spirit

The Holy Spirit is preeminent for wisdom.
The Spirit will be our leader.
It will guide us to the straight path.
Our wise forefathers were guided in this way by the One.

The Spirit will lead us along paths most wise.
The Spirit will give us insight of the truth in all teachings.
The Spirit will make strong our energies and our determination to obtain an all-encompassing wisdom.

No power or greatness can compare to the Spirit as a guide of mortals upon their journey.

The Spirit will lead us to learn the eternal laws of the One.
For the glory of the One we will learn to separate what is true from what is false.
We will be led like a pure one to the love of the One.

We will be led to all the glories on the earth, in heaven, on mountains, in plants, and in the waters.

None of these are we to look on with anger.
All were created by the One, and in them He was and is well pleased.
The Spirit will teach us all this and more when we accept it to be our leader to the One.

The Spirit is from our Lord.
It is His auspicious energy.

It is His wish that we accept the leadership of the Spirit that we may live and may not die.

He is a loving Lord who cares for all who desire to come to Him.

To all who keep the law, both young and old alike, He will give happiness.
He will bestow upon us the Spirit to be our energy that we may live.

The Spirit will guard us on all sides.
Those who would threaten us will not be permitted to come near.
The Spirit will never permit a friend and child of the One to be harmed.

The Spirit will ever protect us.
The Spirit will be our aid.
Even from those who would have us worship and live in an improper way the
Spirit will protect us.

The Spirit comes nigh to prosper us in the proper way.
The Spirit is accepting of our desire to live in the proper way.
The Spirit is accepting of our desire to follow the Sacred Way.
The Spirit will envelop us with God's love.

Following the lead of the Spirit we will become well skilled in speech so we
may be of glory to the One.

Following the lead of the Spirit we will become enrichers of mankind.
Following the lead of the Spirit we will become healers of disease.
Following the lead of the Spirit we will become dispensers of knowledge and
wisdom of the One.

The Spirit is a good friend to us when we follow its lead.

The Spirit will bring happiness to our heart.
The Spirit will make ours a happy home.

The Spirit is bestowed by the One God upon mortal man,
Not to all but to those in whom He takes delight.
The Spirit is bestowed to those who God considers His friends.
The One God does the mighty sage befriend.

The Spirit will save us from slanderous reproach.
The Spirit will keep us from distress.
The Spirit will be our gracious friend.

With the Spirit as our friend, we will grow and develop until we are great.
From every side the powers of the Spirit will unite in us.
We will become for it a gathering place of strength.
We grow and develop until we become truly worthy to be called sons and daughters of the One.

May the rays of the Spirit grow strong in us.
May the Spirit be our friend and fully illuminate us.
May we give all glory to the One.

May we be found worthy of the immortality bestowed upon us by the Spirit of the One.

May we be found worthy and be of service to the One.
May we be found worthy to be of service to mankind.

May we all invest our worship in the glory of the One.
May we shun the honor of ignorant man and bring honor only to the One.
May we be brave in sharing our love of the One.
May His Spirit always find in us a suitable dwelling place.
May we always find in us His love.

For those who worship the One, the Spirit develops in them an active knowledge.
Skilled in many duties we will honor the One and give glory to our Father.
Whatever we do in the world of work, in our homes, or in our churches, synagogues, or temples, all will be done for the glory and honor of the One.

All life will become sacred to those who follow the lead of the Spirit.

Invincible are those upon whom the One has bestowed His Spirit.
It is always their savior and guard.
In this we should all rejoice.

May the One find us worthy.
May His Spirit dispel the darkness of our ignorance.

May God make ours a God-like spirit.
May His Spirit lead ours.
May we let no one nor anything lead us astray.
May we find we are always encompassed by His love.

# The Spirit Has Raised

The Spirit has raised its banner.
It has made its presence known through out the whole earth.
Nevertheless ignorant men continue to prepare their weapons for war.
On ward they go, willing to turn our rivers red with the blood of their kin.

Mankind has chosen to take upon itself the yoke of anger and hatred.
This they have erroneously reasoned to be the easy yoke to bear.
Despite the promptings of the Spirit, mankind has chosen to remain blind in sight and unable to hear.

The red veil of anger and hatred has shut them off from the Spirit of the One.
They take their darkness to be the light.

Few remain, very few indeed, who are active in their task to return mankind to their common path.

Few remain who have accepted the Spirit of the One.
These few accomplish all they do for the glory of the One.

The Spirit will remain ever active to give mankind the opportunity to turn their darkness into light.

The Spirit will remain to bring the light of knowledge for all the world.
It stands ready to enlighten all who would depart from the darkness of ignorance and enter into the Holy Life.

Once beheld, the Spirit removes the veils that have kept us in darkness.
Those who attain to her enter the world of wondrous splendor.

Once we accept the Spirit into our life the veil of darkness will forever depart.
We will enter into the world of clear perception.
We will come face to face with the One.

We will awaken from our slumber.
We will be filled with joy.

The ancient teachers and sages praised the Spirit of the One.
They praised it for planting within us the voice of the One.
When we listen to this voice we will receive charm.
We will receive conspicuous strength to do what needs to be done.

We will be lead onward by the strength of the Spirit that we have received.
We will receive ample knowledge and wisdom to bravely do what needs to be done.

The Spirit of the One envelops all the world.
It does not matter if you are in the east or the west, the north or the south; wherever you may be the Spirit is there.

Whatever you may be doing, the Spirit is there with you.
She is there waiting for you to awaken.
Make no mistake, she hears and understands the voice of each adorer of the One.

Since the most ancient of days, the Spirit has been born anew each day.
Each day she has had to watch most of humankind wasting their lives away.

She has within her power to remove forever the ignorance of man.
She has within her power to display to us the full splendor of the One.
Yet she must watch the diminishing of the days of human creatures.

The Blessed One has only permitted her to extend her rays and her blessings to those who call to Him with their love.

Never will she transgress the divine commands.
She must wait for the man or woman to turn to begin their journey home to the One, their Father.

She waits to bestow her aid, her ample treasure of knowledge and wisdom.
She waits for the man or the woman to truly realize that they are children of the One.
She waits to bestow upon us her wondrous gifts.

May she come to us all very soon.
May she fill us with her sweet sounds.
May she come and fill us with the wealth of knowledge and wisdom.
May the Spirit be with us day and night to guide our way.

May she bring us to experience the full love of the One.

When will we put aside our foolish and ignorant ways?
When will we allow the Spirit to be our guide?
When will we allow the Spirit to animate us?
When will we allow the Spirit to give her light to man?

The Spirit stands ready to give her light to man.
The Spirit stands ready to give us of her strength.

Awaken now.
Accept the Spirit from the One.
Become a health-giver.
Become a wonder-worker for the One.

# The Earth and the Spirit

The Earth and the Spirit are a mighty pair.
They will graciously hearken to our call.
They will accept those who are friendly and wise.
They will prosper those who come to them with their love.

To the person who honors them, they will bestow heroic strength.
They will give that person increase day by day.

They will guard and protect us all the days of our life if we come to them with
love.
They will give us the energy and strength to do the work assigned by the One.

They will not allow those who truly love the One to suffer or be harmed.
They will guide those who love to become brilliant single lights for the many.

From curse and from reproach we will be freed.
We will be released by the Spirit, and the Earth from the fetters which bound
us because of our ignorant and foolish ways.

When we come to the One with our Holy prayer we will be strengthened by
the Spirit and the Earth, so that we may proceed on the way.

Make no mistake upon this point.
The Spirit and the Earth are inseparable parts of the One.
They are both parts of the One.
They are to us as our Father and Mother.
Both desire our honor.

Accept this fact, that both come from and are provided to us by the One.
Let it be pleasing to you.

This will provide to you good protection and kind favor.
When both become sacred to you, you will be granted health and the richness of knowledge and wisdom.

We honor the Spirit and the Earth with a God-devoted heart.
The One protects those who dwell in a sacred way.
The One frees them from distress and grants to you great felicity.

The two, the Spirit and the Earth, must be used together by us in harmony.
When we bring them together as parts of the One, our hymns, our prayers, our actions, and our words will all be accepted by the One.

When we bring all together in harmony we will be counted as being among the Children of the One, as a child of God.

The Spirit and the Earth will bring to those who worship the One their ample recompense.

The Spirit and the Earth are well pleased with those who bring their love to the One.
They will come together in harmony for those who love the One.

They will grant to us mighty powers which none can overcome.
They will bring us an abundance of knowledge and wisdom.
They will cause all our Holy rites to be successful.
They will work in harmony with us on the Sacred Way.

# The One Is Worthy

The One is worthy of our praise.
The One is worthy of our worship.
Will we frame in our minds this thought as a eulogy, as our guiding principle?
Will we place ourselves in his assembly for our good?
Will we place ourselves in His care?

With the friendship of the One, we will not suffer harm.

The men and women who make their life sacred and live in trust of the One
will dwell without a foe.

He or she will gain heroic might.
Day by day they will be strong.
Distress will never approach them.
The One will not let them suffer harm.

May the power of the One be kindled in you.
May all your kind and loving thoughts be fulfilled.
May the One guide you with His love.
May you live your life in an acceptable way.
May the One be with you so that you will not suffer harm.

Let us remind each other of the proper way.
Let us strive to be successful in all that we do.
Let us fill our thoughts with love of the One so that we prolong our lives and
are acceptable to the One.

With the friendship of the One we will not suffer harm.

Let the ministers of the One come forth.
Let them be guardians of the common folk.

Let them work in harmony with the Spirit and the Earth for the good of all mankind.
Let them be mighty heralds of the One.
Let them be dear friends of the One and not suffer harm.

In each generation, a great High Priest takes birth.
This Priest presents to all the truth of the One.
This Priest invokes only the One, the Director of all that is.
This Priest is a purifier of teachings that have been presented in error.
Knowing all priestly work, they work to perfect the teachings and rites like a Sage.
They have the friendship of the One and will not suffer harm.

The One God sees us through even the darkness of the night caused by our ignorance.
Even when we perceive Him as being far removed from us; He is nigh to us, He is close at hand.

His love will encompass us.
When we accept His friendship we will suffer no harm.

With the One foremost in our heart, thoughts, and mind, no evil-hearted man will prevail against us.

The One will attend to our speech and make it prosper well.
We will not, with His Friendship, suffer harm.

With our words we will overcome those who are evil of speech and thought, whether they be near by or far away.

We will be free to live and follow the sacred way.
The One will let none cause us harm.

When we accept the One's yoke of love we will be guided on the Middle Way.
The Spirit will guide each step of the way.
With its friendship we will not suffer harm.

Following the guidance of the Spirit, the way will become easy for us.
We will not suffer harm.

The One has the power to soothe all disharmonies.
The One has the power to overcome all wrath, anger, and hatred.
He will be gracious to us when we let our hearts be turned to Him again.
With His Friendship we will not suffer harm.

The One is our God and our wondrous Friend.
He is fair to all who strive to walk and live in the sacred way.
Under His own protection may we dwell when we turn to Him.
He will not in His friendship allow us to suffer harm.

This is His grace that when we turn to Him and make our hearts His abode,
we will be filled with the Holy Spirit.

The Voice of His Spirit will serve as our guide.
We will be given the vast treasure of knowledge and wisdom.
We will have His friendship and not suffer harm.

May we be counted as Children of the One.
May we have the One dwelling within our hearts and minds.
May we be among the children who are granted freedom from every sin with
perfect wholeness.

May we be the children who are given the strength to dwell in the Holy Way.

May we be they, the Children of the Eternal One.

The One who is all-Good, the One who is our God is here and will lengthen
the days of our existence when we turn to Him.

May the Spirit and the Earth bear witness that we are worthy to be considered
His Sons and His Daughters.

May the One grant this, our prayer.

# To Fair Goals

To fair goals travel the Two, the Spirit and the Earth.
They seem totally unlike, but each in turn nourishes us.
One provides us with the appropriate energy and the other maintains and supports our form.

We are born to be in harmony with the two.
Each has its proper function for the proper development and growth of mankind.
Each provides us with its splendor.

They both deserve our honor.
The One has established them in His proper order.

Who of you knows this secret?
Who of you knows the One who has established all in order?
Who of you has realized that both are necessary for mankind to develop to its own true nature?

Who has realized they are both necessary for us to develop our God-like nature?

The earth is visible and fair.
We grow in its native brightness.
The spirit energizes us and uplifts us so that we may develop in the proper way.

Many are frightened by this and deny that they are born of two apparently different worlds.

When in time they turn to the One and have reverence for Him, they will be led to understand, the two are parts of the One.

These two auspicious ones tend to the development of man.
They each have their proper function and manner.
The One, the Lord of all, has provided us with each one so that we may learn
to harmonize the whole and proceed in the proper manner.

Like a Savior, the One encircles with His arms and with His awesome might
maintains the harmony of the two world's borders.

He maintains each for and in its proper place.
This we need to understand.

The One has made for a most noble form so that we may understand His
splendor.
The One has made this earth our home.
The One has made this earth His home.
The Sage adores the wisdom and knowledge that we receive from the Spirit.
The Sage has realized that this earth is the meeting place where the One is to
be worshiped and experienced.

The Mighty One resides with us.
His kindness and His love preserve us.
Nothing that we do will ever diminish the One.

When we are foolish or act in ignorant ways we do not do harm to the One.
We harm ourselves and our home.

May we grasp this teaching.
May we learn and develop in the proper way.
May we learn to honor the Spirit and the Earth.
May we live in love of the One and in love for each other.
Grant this our prayer.

# The Individual

The individual man or woman who commits to follow the ancient way, is by strength engendered.

Straight away they are encompassed by all wisdom.
The Spirit of the One will encircle them.
They will become one of its friends.
They will possess the wealth-bestowing spirit.

The Ancient One by His word and His call gave all of mankind their being.
He established the heavens and the earth and all that is contained in them.
The One is the bestower of the Spirit to those who walk in the Ancient Way.

Praise the One who is the most ancient of all.
Honor those who commit to His ancient way.
Honor those who make their life a sacred trust.
Honor those who love the One.
These sons and daughters are well tended to by the constant giver.
They become like gods when they accept the life-giving spirit.

The ancient One is rich in the treasure of knowledge.
He is rich in the wealth of wisdom.
He provides these to those He considers His Children.
He set for each of His children a pathway for them to follow.
He guides them with His Spirit.
He is the guard of those who are considered His children.
He is the Father of all upon the earth and all who are in the heavens.

Mankind is like infants who must be nourished day and night.
Without the Spirit to nourish them they will lose their way.
For this reason the Spirit is always available to them to guide them on the way.

Little by little the Spirit gives to them from its treasures.
Only as they develop and learn in the proper way is more given to them.
Only as they strive to learn the sacred way do they develop.
The Spirit is the root of all their wealth.
It is the gathering place of all the treasures.
It is the one that is capable of granting their every wish.
The One has appointed the Spirit the task of preserving humankind as they share in His own immortal life.

Now as in days of old, the ultimate home of all is with the One.
It is He who permitted the ideas of old to be born and those that are born today.
He is the guard of what is and what will be here after.

May the One permit us to draw from His knowledge and wisdom.

May the One grant to us teachers, sages, and priests to guide those who wish to learn in the ancient way.

May He grant us sustenance and lengthen our days so that we may develop and grow in the proper way.

May His Spirit be with us always as we endeavor to find our way.

May the Spirit guide us to the Sacred Way.

May the One grant this our prayer.

# May the Light

May the light of the Spirit of the One chase our ignorance away.
May it bestow upon us knowledge and wisdom.
May this light chase our ignorance and sins away.

May this light provide us with good fields of endeavor.
May this light grant to us pleasant homes.
May this light guide us in the sacred way.
May this light chase our ignorance away.

May we be praisers of the One.
May He permit us to know the sacred way.
May His light chase our ignorance away.

May we be His true worshipers.
May we live as His sons and daughters.
May He take our ignorance away.

May He encompass us on every side with His splendor.
May He encompass us with His love.
May He drive our ignorance away.

May the One look upon us favorably in every way.
May He take us by the hand and guide us past all the obstacles we perceive in
our way.

May He carry us when we are feeling tired or become afraid.
May He take our ignorance away.

# It Is the Grace

It is by the grace of the One that we continue to exist.
He is the Lord Supreme over all living things.
He has brought us all to this life.
He looks with interest on all we do.
He has no rival, although we do not perceive this or comprehend.

The One is present in the heavens.
The One is present in the earth.
The One is present in all things.
He provides us with His vigor.
He is present with us at all times.
He preserves us day and night.
He preserves us despite our ignorant and foolish ways.
He is protecting us although we do not perceive this or comprehend.

May it forever be true that the One will look favorably upon us.
May His Spirit, His Wisdom, His Knowledge, and His Love forever encircle
us.
May we always be in His care.
May the One grant this our prayer.

# For the Sake of Mankind

For the sake of mankind let us press to be bestowed with the Holy Spirit.

May the One permit the Spirit to enlighten us.

May the One permit the Spirit to drive our malignant thoughts away.

May the One carry us through all our troubles.

May the One guide us through our grief.

May the One develop and strengthen us so that we may be truly worthy to be called His sons and daughters.

May the One grant this our prayer.

# Our True Home

Our true home is with the One.
Our Father is the Mighty One, the Lord of Strength.
He is the King Supreme of the earth and the heavens.
He is the Lord of all true power.
It is He we are to invoke whenever we are in need.

The Way of the One seems unattainable to us.
Although we do not realize it He is with us in everything we do.
He is the One who protects us when we do things in foolish ways.
He shows His mighty ways to those who are His Friends and endeavor to
follow the Sacred Way.

Whatever paths we choose to take, the One may be found there.
Those who choose the Sacred Way will experience His great resistless might.
He will provide the strength, knowledge, and wisdom to over come any
obstacle we perceive.

To those who would be rulers, He is the Supreme Ruler.
To those who would be friends, He is the Friend beyond compare.
He is the Praiser in the midst of praisers.
He is the One honored most by singers.
He is the wordsmith of our most Holy thoughts.

Despite His great strength He treats us as His own children.
He could consume us but He protects us even when we behave in foolish
ways.
He is our closest comrade and is always prompting us to do good deeds.

He is the humbler of the prideful.
He is the terminator to those who excite conflict.

He is the Lord of those who would do heroic deeds.
He is the God invoked by many who do not truly know Him.
He overlooks our foolishness this day.
He guides us through our foolishness that we may, one day, come to travel in the proper way.

His help has made us successful.
He has given us cheer and provides us with comfort.
He is the guardian of our way.
We may not realize it but He is with us each day.
He is the sole Lord of all.
He is the Lord of every Holy service.
He is with us every day.

Those who are true Heroes have received their strength from Him.
He helps all who come to the aid of mankind when there is trouble.
The light of His Spirit may be found even in our darkest hour.
He may be found at our side even when we have been blinded by the darkness caused by our ignorant and foolish ways.

With His left hand He can control and overcome even those who are mighty in their evil ways.

With His right hand He will gather and protect all who are striving to learn and travel by a sacred way.

Even the humble and the feeble may acquire the wisdom and knowledge of the sacred way.

Well known is He today by all the people.
The rich know Him and the poor know Him.
Even those who express their hate for His ways know Him.
Mark my words; they who hate Him will be overcome.

He is the One invoked by many.
His ways are known by our kinsmen.
His ways are known by those we look upon as strangers.
He is with all who worship, although we may not approve of their ways.

With the Holy Spirit He guards all the people of the earth.
It is He who is awesome and mighty.
It is He who provides the inhabitants of the earth with boundless knowledge.
It is He who is honored in our words and songs.

Will you be one of those who win the bestowal of His Holy Spirit?
Will you be one of those who find that you have His voice within?
Will you be one of those who receive His rich gifts and treasures?
Will you dedicate your life to His service?
Will you commit to live in the Sacred Way?

The One maintains our eternal home with His strength.
He surrounds us on every side.
The heavens and the earth are His.
They are within His control.
They are a small part of His abode.
May He delight with our service.
May He save us from our foolish ways.
May He teach us to honor the Spirit and the Earth.

We do not fully comprehend the limitless power of the One.
As mortal men we are powerless as compared to Him.
As mortal men we have not yet partaken in the Water of Life, which comes from Him.

He far surpasses our loftiest conceptions.
He surpasses the heavens and the earth.

Despite our limitations and our misconceptions He treats us as His own children.
He takes note of what we do and say.

It is this Mighty One, Our Father, that we hope to please.
May He never exclude us from His fellowship.

He is the much-invoked One.
He will lay low those who try to lead His children astray.
He is the Mighty One who is always true with His Friends.

May the One evermore be our protector and guide.
May we evermore live in a way that will make us worthy of being considered
His children.

May he grant this, our prayer.

# We Worship

We worship the One God. To Him we give our praise.
To the One we say our prayers. Of the One we sing our hymns.
It is He we ask for help. It is He we ask to be our friend.

The One does not help the unrighteous ones.
His aid is for those who He considers His friends.
He allows distress to come to those who turn their backs on Him.
We invoke Him always to be our friend.

The One's great work is beyond manly might.
He has established the heavens and the earth.
He will maintain all who keep His Holy Law.
He has established all of nature's laws.
We invoke Him to be our friend.

The One is the Lord and Master of all.
He is the One we honor with our words and praise.
He is the firm and sure One.
He is the Lord and establisher of every Holy Act.
He is with all who give to Him their love.
We invoke Him to be our friend.

The One is the Lord of all the world.
He is the Lord of all that moves and breathes.
He has existed since before all time began.
He has made and established all.
We invoke Him to be our Friend.

Cowards try to invoke Him when they flee.
Men of War try to invoke Him when they are ready to fight.

All turn to the One to come to their aid.
The One is with those individuals who hold Him in their constant thought.
He will aid those who have shown Him their love.
The One we invoke to be our friend.

If you go to the lowest region, the One will be found there.
If you go to the boundary of heaven, the One will be found there.
Our hymns of praise extol the One, the far renowned.
With our love, we invoke Him to be our Friend.

The One God responds when we come to Him with our love.
We may live in a palace. We may live in a slum.
We may be feeble or strong. We may be rich or poor.
He will come to us when we go to Him in love.
If you worship, pray, speak, or sing, do it all with love.

We seek to know the One. We seek to be strong.
We seek to receive the Holy Spirit.
We seek to have answers to our prayers.
If you wish to find and receive what you seek,
If you wish to rejoice with the One in your life,
You must first turn to Him with your love.

Do you wish to have a joyful life?
Do you wish to know the proper words to speak?
Do you wish to be a doer of many good deeds?
The One will be gracious to you. The One will be pleased.
The One will show you the way when you turn to Him with love.

The One guards the assembly of those who are His worshipers.
He guards those who have come to Him with their love.
Our prayers will be granted when we come to Him with love.
He will guide us when we do all we do with love.

# To the One

To the One God I will bring my words.
To the One God I will bring my praise.
He will find these acceptable for I bring them all with love.
The One God is He who will share with me His strength.
The One God is He who will bestow the Holy Spirit when He is well pleased.

In every region of this earth, the glory of the One may be seen.
In all the heavens and beyond, the glory of the One may be seen.
He has established and maintains the cycles and times of all.
As we run the course of life we may behold that He has shared His guidance
and instruction with all.

He has established and maintains all. In this we may have faith.

May He grant to share with us His knowledge.
May He grant to share with us His joy.
May He grant to us shelter from the troubles of life.
He, the One, will do these things when we have demonstrated our love.

He is our encourager. He is always at our side.
He is our aid and our guide.
He bestows on us joy and felicity.
He, the One, does all these things when we have demonstrated our love.

Mankind has invented many ways to try to win His aid.
Mankind has invented many ways to try to get His treasures.
The One has fixed His mind to aid none except those who demonstrate their
love.
With love alone may all the bounties of the One be obtained.

The One's arms encircle mankind.
The One is the bestower of boundless power.
He aids us to do our best in our acts of love.
He helps us to do our best in a hundred ways.
The One is mighty in strength. None may rival Him.
He is eager to help all the people who call on Him.
He is eager to help when we come to Him with love.

The glory of the One is a thousand times greater than what we can conceive.
He stands in our midst, and yet we do not know.
His boundless spirit surrounds us, and yet we do not see.

Of the great might, which is with us, we do not conceive.
In the whole world and above, the One has no foe.
By nature, from days of old, the One has been in all.

We call Him the first of the gods. He is the mighty One.
May the One fill with spirit this lover's heart.
This is my prayer.

The One will prevail.
The One will overcome all obstacles for those who share their love.
He will open our eyes and our ears when we have opened our hearts to Him.
He will open our eyes and our ears when we have opened our minds to Him.
With His aid we will overcome every perceived foe.

May the One evermore be our protector and guide.
May the One look favorably on us and grant this prayer.

# Many Teach

Many teach that the One is far distant from man.
Many teach that all He could ever teach to man was taught to the Sages of Old.
Many teach the One controls the heaven but another reigns upon the earth.
These two will always meet in battle, is what they teach.
Such teachings have led to much foolishness in man.
Such teachings have continued the ignorance of man.

The One established the whole earth and the heavens too.
He firmly fixed the earth, the air, and the waters for the good of mankind.
He established the earth to be our home.

Armed with this knowledge, and trusting in the One,
We may wander the earth and see that this is true.
We may know that the One has made His home with us.
We may know that His might and His glory will ever increase in those who share His love.

Shame comes to all who separate the One from man.

To those who teach that the One forever resides with the human race will be eternal glory.

To those who lead others to the sacred way of the One will be given the name, "Children of God."

All about us we can see the abundant wealth of the One.
All about us we can see He possesses all knowledge and wisdom.
We can trust in the One's great spirit to be with us and guide us when we turn to Him with love.

Everywhere we look, we can see the wonders of God.

To those who truly love Him,
To those who seek to serve mankind with love,
He will pour out to them His Holy Spirit.
They may then be called, "Children of God."

The One watches over His children.
He protects them from those who are godless.
He will prosper their way.

When will mankind awaken?
When will they see it does not prosper them to try to separate the One from man?
When will we awaken from our slumber?

When will mankind acknowledge that the One is their Father and Friend?

May we awaken from our slumber.
May we take delight in knowing we are all One.
May we experience the joy of the Sacred Way.
May we rejoice as we turn back to the One.
May the One, grant this our prayer.

# Mankind Has Made

Mankind has made altars of stone and wood for God.
We say God is present at these altars.
We say they are His resting place and His home.
Day and night mankind comes to these altars to pay homage to their God.

These men come to their God for assistance.
Why does He not come quickly to their aid?
Why does He not come quickly upon these pathways made by man?
Why does He not come to lead these people to a happy life?

Mankind's worship in this way is truly nothing but wishful thinking.
Man has wandered from the Sacred Way.
May they awaken from their slumber before they drown in the sea established
by their own ignorance.

May mankind awaken and change their foolish ways.

We must awaken to our kinship with the One.
We must awaken to our kinship with all of mankind.
We must awaken to the presence of the One who is with us wherever we
might be.
We must awaken to the One in whom we live.
We must awaken to His being within us.
We must awaken to His Holy Spirit that never rests.
We must awaken to His rule in everything we do.

As soon as we awaken, the traces of the One will be discovered everywhere.
We will know that the One is in our home.
We will know His dwelling in our heart.
We will know His dwelling in our mind.

Now think about this if you will.
The One is with you wherever you are.
He is with you in whatever you think, say, or do.

The One will give us a share of His Spirit when we awaken and do all we do with love.

The One will be with us as we walk in the Sacred Way.
The One will purify us and lead us to sinlessness.
The One will do us no harm.
The One will allow no harm to come to us, when we travel the Sacred Way.
Our trust is in His mighty Spirit to guide us into the proper way.
As we place our trust in the One, He will lead us on.
He will bestow upon us only what we are prepared to receive.
He will not come to us if we are unready to accept His love and travel the Sacred Way.

Even in our ignorant and foolish ways, He will not slay us.
He will not forsake us.
He will allow us to experience the consequences of our own foolishness.
He will wait to bestow upon us the knowledge and wisdom, which could be ours, till we are ready.

He will take delight in us and aid us when we turn to Him with our love.
He will show us that He and His Spirit have always been within us, waiting for us to awaken from our slumber.

When we awaken, the One will come to us.
He will bestow upon us the Spirit to guide us in the proper way.
He has always been within us, to awaken to and discover.
When we awaken and call to Him with our love, He will hear us and be to us a Father and Friend.

# In Our Deep Distress

In our deep distress we call on the One for aid.
In our most difficult situations He will come and rescue us.

He will aid us to overcome all our foes.
He will bring us to full prosperity.
He will bring us joy.

Our most glorious Father will aid us.
Our Mother too will give us strength.
They will rescue us from distress when we follow their law.

We pray to the One who is ruler over men.
We pray and sing our hymns.
We pray to share in His strength and might.
We pray that He will rescue us from all distress.

We pray that He will make for us an easy path.
We crave His aid that we may find rest with Him.
We crave to receive the love that He has for men.

When by our foolishness we sink into the pit,
We call to the One for aid.
When difficulties arise, we call for the One to rescue us.

May He guard us with His power and might.
May He keep us within His ceaseless care.
May He grant this prayer of ours.
May He guide and instruct us in the proper way.

# When We Walk

When we walk in the sacred way we will obtain the acceptance of the One.
We will obtain His favor.
He will deliver us from all troubles.

When our words and our songs exalt the One He will be pleased.
The One will be with us and grant us His protection.
With His powers around us we will find safe shelter.

When our works are done, and He finds pleasure in them,
He will grant our prayer.

May the world take note that we serve the One and walk within the Sacred
Way.

# The One Looks

The One looks upon all living things.
Upon the Sacred Way we should take our stand.
We should come together and drink from the Holy Spirit provided by Him.

As vast as this world of ours seems to be,
The Spirit of the One is greater and more far-reaching.
Partake of the Spirit till your soul is over flowing.

Let us be blessed by the One together.
Let us strive with one aim, which is to be found worthy by Him.
Let us be in harmony with the Spirit and be called Children of the One.

Let us stand together and express our love of the One.
Let our works speak for us of our love.
Let us draw the Holy Spirit around us and within us.
May the One be with us and display to us His favor.

Many brave deeds may be accomplished as we serve the One.
He will share with us His strength and might.
May His ancient and auspicious bonds of friendship be with us forever.
May we always be permitted to share the Holy Spirit.

We do not have to contend with anyone to receive this Holy Spirit.
It is free flowing to all who come with true conviction.
It is free to all who love God and perform a loving service to mankind.

When we invite the Spirit into our dwelling place,
When we express and show our love of the One,
The One will rejoice with us and bestow upon us His Spirit.

It matters not what is your nationality or tribe.
It matters not what your declared religion may be.
If you serve mankind with love and love the One,
The Holy Spirit will fill you to overflowing.

It does not matter where you live, in the east or the west, the north or the south, or the central regions.

If you love the One and serve mankind with love,
The Holy Spirit will fill you to overflowing.

No one may prevent the Holy Spirit from coming to you but you.
The mightiest men upon the earth cannot prevent the Spirit from coming to you.
Take delight that the One will be pleased with you, if you express your love to Him and serve mankind with love.

His Holy Spirit will fill you to overflowing.

If you want to be considered as a child of the One, come and partake in the Sacred Way.

If you want to be filled with knowledge and wisdom, come and partake in the Sacred Way.

If you love the One and serve mankind with love,
You will be filled with the Holy Spirit to overflowing.

Come now if you are willing.
No one can prevent you from becoming a child of the One.

Love the One.
Serve Mankind with love.
Be filled with the Holy Spirit to overflowing.

# Longing for Support

Longing for support I have looked around to see if there are any who share the same spirit or dream.

I have looked for kinsmen and brothers of the Way, but none would openly come forward.

I have found support only with the One.
His providence has cared for me.

The One has cared for me.
He is closer to me than my nearest kin.
All my love I share with Him.
To Him I sing my praise.

I have accepted the offer of His Spirit. I will not turn from His Way.

No one may break the cord that ties me to the One.
When I strove to gain the powers, of which our forefathers wrote,
The One filled me with His Spirit. He filled me till I could receive no more.
The One is to me my Father.

The One has been prepared to give to all His divine guidance.
He has been prepared to bestow His Holy Spirit to all who come.
With His hands and arms He waits to welcome all who will come.
He is ready for you to taste the sweetness of the Spirit.

The One is the mightiest of all.
He waits to guide you in living a sacred life.
With Him at your side you will be ever active.
He will fill you with His Spirit and give you delight.

The Spirit surpasses the strength of all men combined.
The Spirit exceeds the heavens and the earth in greatness.
The Spirit of the One is greater than all things.

The One with His Spirit protects those who walk on the Sacred Way.
The Wealth of knowledge and wisdom the One may bestow is beyond anything we can measure.

It is true that our forefathers were united with the One through this same Spirit.
The One offers this same Spirit to us to guide us and aid us as we walk in His Holy Way.

# It Is Time

It is time for the Holy Work to be which was done in ancient times to be done again.
Mankind has created a sea full of gods.
It is time to offer the Spirit of the One to man with the hallowing word.

Most of mankind has wandered from the Holy Way into paths, which will lead only to destruction.

Many are claiming to be Children of God but are traveling further and further from their Home.

The One wants His children to make the journey to their home.
He wants them to return by the pathway of love.

Our savior, our Father, has given to mankind the opportunity for immortality.
We are to proclaim Him, the One, from whom none can hide.
He has again given us the opportunity to drink from His chalice if we will but return.

He is not a three-fold god or a four-fold god as some claim Him to be.
He is the One, there is no other. He is the One our ancestors called "I am."

When they served Him with love,
When they served the One as Priests and lived in the sacred way,
They, although they were mortal, they gained immortality.

He wants His children now to return by the Sacred Way.

Search your hearts; pray for what is best.
See if these, His words, ring true.
He is waiting for us to return to the ancient Sacred Way.

Come as near as you can. Return to the way of our Father.

Return to the giver of knowledge and wisdom.
Return home to your Father. He is waiting to welcome you.
He is ready to bestow His favor on you and give you happiness beyond compare.
Those who do not return will wander further and further from the way.

Become a child again of the One.
Join with the Spirit and become youthful again.

Accept the Spirit, the Strength, and the Might of the One.
Become His Child again.

# Working with Skill

Working with skill, renew mankind's knowledge of God.
Renew their awareness of His Holy Spirit.
Make full use of the great gifts the One has bestowed on you.
Make them aware of their Parents, the Spirit, and the Earth.
Make them aware that they may make life young again.
It is within your power.

Within us is the ability to make all life Sacred again.
Within us is the active vital power.
Within us is the skill and wisdom as noble children of the One.
He has granted this power most excellent to His children.
As a family we may grow and prosper all upon the earth.

The One has made prosperity for us.
He has provided us with knowledge and wisdom.
He has let us know that there are not strangers and kin.
He has let us know we are all one family.
He has provided for us the Way.

The One, our Lord, I invoke for aid.
It is He who will end the spirit drought.
He will speed us to knowledge and wisdom.
He will provide us with all that we need.
He has provided for us the Way.

The One has provided what we need to overcome all obstacles.
He will prosper and protect us as we follow the Way.

The heavens and the earth are a school for us.
We graduate by following the Holy Way.

May the One continue to guide us.
This is our prayer.

# Honor Our Mother and Father

Honor our Mother and our Father, the Spirit and the Earth.
See how they glow when they are brought together.
Approach them both with love and care.
They provide you with ample tools for the journey we call life.

Ample and unfailing are their aids.
Whatever you may think, they are here to give us care and aid.
They will come together for us in the proper way.
They will help us to see things in the proper way.
They will aid us in all our Holy acts.

With the Holy Spirit you will seem as a supreme lord.
The common folk may even want to worship you.
This you are not to permit.
You received the Spirit to aid and guide them.
You are not the god, even though it is within your power to make a barren cow
give milk.

Your task is to aid the wanderers through their journey of life.
Your task is to guide and teach them of the Sacred Way.
You are to teach them the power of love.
You are to teach them to live in harmony with the earth.
You are to teach them how they, too, may receive the Spirit.

All mankind has been raised from the waters.
They have been bound and imprisoned by foolish ways.
You are to bring them from the darkness caused by ignorance.
You are to bring them to the light of knowledge and wisdom.
You are to be their aid.

Raise mankind from the pit caused by their arrogant and foolish ways.
Be an unfailing help and guide to those who wish to learn.
Comfort them in their woe and show them the Holy Way.
Aid those who are willing to end their foolish ways.

Show those who are willing how to have a happy home.
Show those who are willing the friendship given to the Children of the One.
Raise those who are willing from the fiery pit.
Guard each one as you would a child while they learn the Way.

The Mighty One has placed within you many powers.
He has given you the ability to give sight to the blind.
He has given you the ability to make the lame to walk.
He set you at liberty from your past mistakes.
He set you here to be of aid to those who seek the Holy Way.

You may have the power to control the mighty waters.
You may have the power to always live in comfort.
You may have the power to preserve your body from decay.
Your power is to be used to aid others who need your help.

You are to help those who seek the Holy Way.
You are to help in a thousand ways.
You are to help those who feel powerless to change their foolish way.
You are to be a friendly guard of those who need aid.

Be a bountiful giver to all who wish to learn the Sacred Way.
Share with them your knowledge.
Share with them your wisdom.
Guide those who are willing to find their way Home.

Come to the aid of all who are willing.
Guide them if they are willing.
Show them love and forbearance as they search for their way.
Stand always willing to aid those who are willing.

Teach them of the Spirit that surrounds them.
Teach them that the One is not far away.

Teach them how to live in harmony with their land.
Protect those who need your help.
Come to them with your aid.

Protect and guard well those who want to come into the Holy Way.
Those who remain in ignorance and those who persist in their foolishness
may be slain by their own misguided deeds.

With those who turn their back on Holy guidance, turn from them.
Leave them to suffer from the consequences of the own foolishness.

Honor those who seek to receive the Spirit.
Honor those who seek their home with the One.
Come to them with your aid.

Deliverance is vouchsafed to all who seek to abandon their foolish ways.
They will receive favor and guidance as they search for the Way.
Each whose heart and mind are willing will receive aid.

You have the majesty of the One within your form.
You may find it if you will look within.
He will set your course like kindling a fire.
Stay the course and you will be helped with His mighty aid.

Fill your heart with love.
Through love the Mighty Spirit will be liberated.
It will flow through you to all.
You will be helped.
You will be given new strength.
You will become a guide to those who are searching.

You will be wed to the Spirit of the One.
You will freely give to all who are truly in need.
You will become a kind host to those who are taking the journey.

The One will bring great bliss to those who share their love.
He will give them great gifts.
He will give protection and aid to those who are gracious and good.

Those who serve God and their fellow man will be helped in the race of life.
They will be given the strength of the young.
They will be given knowledge and wisdom, which is reserved for the wise.
They will receive a thousand aids.

In all strife they will be kept safe from harm.
They will be safely guarded by the One.

The Lord of a hundred powers will be their guardian and protector.
He will give them strength beyond the comprehension of mortal man.
He will be with them in all they do.
He will be with them wherever they may go.

The One will make your speech effectual.
The words you speak will be as if they were His own.
The One will make you a mighty wonder worker.
He will give you the wisdom and the knowledge to do all things.
You will be a child to Him,
A Child in whom He is well pleased.

With undiminished blessings, you will be protected, both in the night and in the day.
You will love the One, your God.
You will love and serve your fellow man.

May you accept the responsibility that is now yours.
May the One be with you every day.

# The Light of the Spirit

The Light of the Spirit has come.
It is the fairest of all lights.
It is the most brilliant and far extending.
The night of ignorance is sent away.
It yields its place to the Light.

The fair, bright Spirit brings its offspring.
Wisdom and knowledge come with her.
Dark ignorance resigns when they arrive.
Both are kin following each other.

Common and unending is the pathway.
Taught to all by the One, alternately they travel.
Fair formed and one minded, they do not clash, nor do they tarry.

The bright Spirit is our leader.
We hear her sounds, and our eyes behold her.
She stirs up the world.
She awakens every living creature.

The bright Spirit awakens the sleeper.
She awakens one for enjoyment.
She awakens one for wealth.
She awakens one for worship.
She extends our vision so that we may see great wonders.

She awakens one to high position.
She awakens one to exalted glory.
She awakens one to pursue gain.
She awakens one to his labor.
All are awakened to their proper vocation.

When we receive this fair Spirit,
We become a true child of the One.
We possess all true treasure.

She is with us for endless morns to come.
We will follow in the proper path.
With Her we become the living.
She awakens the ones who are dead from their slumber.

She causes the love of the One to be kindled.
She reveals to us all of creation.
She awakens men to offer worship.
She performs for the One a noble service.

For a long time wisdom and knowledge shall be together.
Each will come into man at the proper time.
Each will guide men in the proper way.

Gone are the men who in ancient times looked upon the Spirit.
We now are the living.
It is now for us to behold this Spirit.
It is now for us to come to her and take hold of the Spirit.

This Spirit will chase all our ignorance away.
It is born of the Law of the One.
It is the Law's protector.
It is the joy giver to all who take hold of her.

From days eternal has the Spirit brought its light to those who would awaken.
She brings this light to us today.
She will endow us with riches.
Her light will shine on for all the days to come.

She is from the immortal One and moves on in her own proper course.
She is undecaying.

The Spirit has shown forth the splendor of the One.
She has thrown off the veil of dark ignorance.

She awakens the world.
She awakens all who are willing.

The Spirit brings to us life-sustaining blessings.
She sends forth her brilliance to all the world.
All who are willing may arise from their slumber.

Arise today. Accept the Spirit.
Accept the breath, the life of the One.
Again today we have been offered the Spirit.
Take hold of it, and the darkness of ignorance will pass away.

She will not leave her path.
She will not come to you unless you are willing.
She will arrive and prolong your life only if you are willing.

Sing your hymns today.
Speak your words of praise.
Become a Priest of the One.
Accept the Spirit's gift of life.
Accept the Spirit's offspring to guide you.

All may become sons and daughters of the One.
All may accept the offering of the Holy Spirit.
All may learn to live a life of love.

Rise now and show Him your devotion.
Commit to living in the Sacred Way.
Commit to living a life of love.

Receive today the blessings of the Spirit.
Offer up your praise in loving worship.
Serve the One and serve mankind.

To you will be vouchsafed life eternal.

# To the Strong One

To the Strong One we bring our words of praise.
He is the Lord and Master of all.
We pray it will be well with all our men.
We pray that in our towns and homes all will be healthy and well fed.

We ask the One to be gracious to us.
We ask the One to bring us joy.
With reverence we will serve the One.
With His guidance we will live a sacred life.

May we by worship of the One gain His grace.
We will praise the Bounteous One, the ruler of all men.
May He come to our families and bring them bliss.
May He keep us uninjured as we walk in the sacred path.

We call the Wise One to come to our aid.
We have wandered far from the Way.
May He lead us back to the sacred path.
We desire His favorable grace.

We call to the One with reverence.
May He fill us full with His medicines.
May He grant us His full protection.
May He provide us with shelter and make our homes secure.

To our Father we address our hymns.
To Him we look for strength and might.
May He grant us food for mortals to eat.
May He be gracious to us and our progeny.

May the One keep us from harm.
May He let not harm either great or small come to us.
May He keep us from the slayer's wrath.
May He teach us to live that we do no harm.

Let no harm come to us or our progeny.
Let us be found among the living.
Let not the consequences of our former ways overtake us.
With our love we will forever more call to and serve the One.

I bring Him my hymns of praise.
The Father of all gives us happiness.
We are blessed with His favor and benevolence.
We receive the saving help from the One.

It is not His intent to let man die.
He desires all men to live in the bliss of His care.
He will be gracious to us and bless us.
He will give protection to all who come to Him.

We are always seeking His help.
We have spoken of Him with great reverence.
We have demonstrated our love.
May He now favor us and hear when we call.

# The Brilliant Presence

The Brilliant presence of the One has risen.
He looks upon all that has been created.
His Spirit fills the air, the earth, and the heavens.
He may be found wherever we may be.

The One is ever with us.
We may be too blind to see.
He searches for the pious men and women.
Those who serve Him will receive a happy fortune.

The Auspicious One will meet with us.
The Spirit will bear to Him our prayers.
All around the earth the One waits to meet with us.
He waits for pious men and women to send Him their prayers.

The One God will not withdraw.
He will not leave His work unfinished.
He has loosed His Spirit.
He has sent it out to encompass the earth.

The Spirit of the One assumes many forms.
It comes to all mankind in a form they may understand.
The One will maintain His eternal power.
He will bring mankind from the darkness of ignorance.
He will bring mankind to His light of knowledge and wisdom.

Each day He delivers us from trouble.
Each day He delivers us from dishonor.
Each day He guides our steps on the Way.
Each day He comes in answer to our prayers.

# Each Day

Each day I speak and write my words of praise.
Each day I send them forth.
Each day they seem to disappear upon the wind.
No one seems to listen or care.

I will continue to express a mighty opinion.
I will continue to trust proudly in the One.
I will continue to run the race of life.
I will trust in the One to overcome all dark ignorance.

As a dead man leaves his riches,
I will leave my dark ignorance behind.
I will ever be animated by the Spirit.
I will travel with the words of the One.

The One God will hold me up.
The One will be with me day and night.
As I travel in the Holy Way,
He will not leave me stranded.

I will go into the darkness.
I will go to where there is no apparent support.
I will go from station to station.
The One will go with me and carry me to His home.

He has given me the teachings of old to deliver.
He has given me the gift of His knowledge and wisdom.
He is ever present with each of us.
He is still worthy of our praise.

The One will give to you knowledge and wisdom.
He will show to you the sacred path.
He will deliver to you the Spirit.
He asks only that you give Him your praise.

The Spirit's fire will keep you from the cold of ignorance.
He will furnish you with the proper nourishment.
He will bring you forth from the cave of foolishness.
He will bring you to the comfort of His Way.

He will bring you to the well.
You will be given to drink from the waters of life.
He will satisfy all your thirst.
He will bring you into His abundance.

From of old, the One has guided men and women.
He has been closer to us than our skin.
He has not left us as helpless babes.
He maintains our life when we turn to Him.

Worthy of our praise and our love is the One.
His Spirit is here for us to win.
He knows full well those who search for His treasure.
He will deliver them from the pit of ignorance.

I will speak always of the mighty deeds of the One.
I will publish all that I have come to know.
As a child of the One I strive to walk in His Way.
I will make known to you the sweetness of His Spirit.

The Lord of many treasures is called "The Wise."
He has given to us one great rite to follow.
As if an order to His children,
He has told us to walk in the Way of Love.

The One will take you from the jaws of death.
When you stand with Him, He will set you free.
As you mourn in your days of trouble,
He will give you the vision to know the Way.

In the dark night of our ignorance,
When we seek to follow a teacher's wild opinions,
He will give you the straight way to follow.
He will open the doors and lead you into the Way.

Our Father will not take away our sight.
He will not allow anyone to slay us.
He will keep us uninjured as we follow the Way.
He is the Great Wonder Worker and Physician.

Strive to be considered His son or daughter.
Strive to reach this lofty goal.
He is within your heart to guide you.
You are never apart from Him.

Return to His house, your home with the One.
He has prepared for you to return.
He has set for you a store of splendid riches.
Return to Him and accept His yoke of love.

Accept His rule, and He will give you wealth.
Accept His rule, and He will give you life.
Accept His love, and He will make you His child.
Accept His love, and the Holy Spirit will be yours.

In our ignorance we seek for the easy path.
We do not see that the Spirit is all around.
We often see God as our foe.
We do not consider the foolishness of our ways.

Each day we prepare for battle.
We go out to gather our spoils with our might.
Misfortune is most often our reward.
Only the One can drive this misfortune away.

You have been given the right to drink,
To drink from the deep well the water of life.

You have been offered a very great might.
You have been offered the help of the Spirit.

Come as sons and daughters, return to the One.
Live as a righteous person. Your powers will be restored.
You need not be like some lost creature.
Your Father stands ready to help His sons and daughters.

Rise from the slumber of your sleep.
Rise to accept the Holy Spirit of the One.
Lay aside the cruel bonds of foolish ways.
Give up suffering affliction. Accept the Waters of life.

I have declared the One's wondrous deeds.
I have declared what I have experienced.
May you find these words of benefit to you.
Even if I enter old age, I will live in my Father's house.

# The Ancient Priests

The Ancient Priests invited us to partake of the Holy Spirit.
The Spirit was said to bring gladness.
It was our gift from the One.
It was apportioned to us as we grew in love and strength.

The Holy Spirit they said was swifter than our thought.
This Sprit comes to us when we call.
This Spirit will make its home within our abode.
It seeks always to welcome and dwell with the pious.

When honored the Spirit frees us from the pit of ignorance.
We become the Children of the One when we accept the Spirit.
We are freed from malignant thoughts and deeds.
They are repelled from us by the Spirit of the One.

The ancient sage has told us that we will become mighty heroes.
We will be given the ability to rescue others from their vile ways.
All may be rescued by the wondrous power of the Spirit.
The deeds done in ancient days we will have the ability to do and more.

You may become a wonder worker for the One.
The Spirit is already available to you, hidden within like buried gold.
You need not remain in your state of slumber.
You need not live in the darkness of ignorant and foolish ways.

You need not wander by paths unknown.
You have it within you to become a Child of the One.
You have it within you to become a leader for your people.
You have it within your power to bring untold blessings to your people.

Become a Child of the One God.
Accept the Spirit from the founder of the royal line.
Publish the good news that all are welcomed when they return.
All are welcomed to become again Children of the One.

Return again to your Father's dwelling.
He will restore to you your full power.
He will restore the Holy Spirit to you.
He will again welcome you as His Child.

You may use the Spirit in many different ways.
At your pleasure you may learn to properly walk in the proper ways.
When you are ready you will learn to use the Spirit.
You will learn a thousand ways to properly use your power.

Learn the many glorious things that are yours.
You will become a bountiful giver of blessing to others.
You will know how to be effective with your powers.
You will be nourished and strengthened with knowledge and wisdom.

Are you ready to be honored as a son or daughter of the One?
Are you ready to show your reverence for the Father?
Are you ready to serve Him with devotion?
Are your ready to accept the responsibility of being His child?

You will be a child of the One wherever you go.
You will be a child of the One whatever you may do.
You will be a child of the One whenever you speak.
You will be a guide for others seeking to return home.

With the aid of your great power you may raise the dead.
With the aid of your great power you may restore youth to an ancient one.
As a child all you do is to bring glory to the One.
Are you ready to bear such great power and responsibility?

You will be forever youthful when you serve the One.
You will bring back to mankind the remembrance of the One.
You will be demonstrating to mankind the Ancient Way.
Are you ready to guide mankind back from its foolish ways?

Invoke the aid of the One in all that you do.
He will carry you and protect you as you journey through the ocean of despair.
His Spirit will come to you swifter than your thought.
His Spirit will carry you back to the safety of His home.

Most of mankind has been blinded by ignorant and foolish ways.
You will have to give them eyes that they may have clear vision.
Most of mankind has become deaf by living in foolish ways.
You will have to give them ears that they may hear and understand.

Bring joy to the blind. Bring joy to the deaf.
Open their eyes and ears to the truths of the Holy Spirit.
Be as a lover to all of mankind.

Great and giving are those children who are aided by the Spirit.
The object of all their thought is to enlighten those who are lost.
With the One to aid them they may make whole the cripple.
Always and in everything they work for the glory of the One.

Are you ready to be a Wonder Worker filled with knowledge and wisdom?
Are you ready to feed mankind with the knowledge and wisdom of the One?
Are you ready to try to replace mankind's barren teachings with the truth of the One?
Are you ready for the powers that come to a child of the One?

Will you prepare the field to receive the true knowledge?
Will you plant the seeds of knowledge and watch it grow?
Will you be a Wonder Worker for your Father?
Will you bring the light of wisdom and knowledge to those who have remained in darkness?

The Holy Spirit has revealed truth to you.
You have become a true child of the One.
You have the ability to be a Wonder Worker.
The secret teachings of the One for His children are now within you.

You are a Sage, a Priest, a Teacher, and a Child of the One.
He will be gracious to you and surround you with His love.
He will be with you to answer all your prayers.
He will be with His children in all they do.

The One has brought you to life again.
He has bestowed on you a liberal bounty.
He has made you His son or His daughter.
Will you live in a Way that is worthy?

Relate to your fellow men all that has been done.
Relate to your brothers and sisters as was done in the days of old.
Show your love to the One.
Do loving service to God and to mankind.
Be a true child and lover.

# Fly with the Spirit

Fly with the Spirit as your guide.
Be most gracious to those who are searching for the way.
Bring your friendly help to all who are in need of guidance.
Come to all with the Holy Spirit to aid them on their way.

Go to all with body, soul, and spirit.
Share with all who are seeking the knowledge and wisdom you have.
Fill them full with knowledge and wisdom.
Lead each to become a child of the One and grow strong.

Be a true wonder worker; be a Child of the One.
Go swiftly with the Spirit to those who suffer affliction.
Follow the teachings of the ancient sage.

Let the Spirit bear you to where there is need.
Take upon you the One's yoke of love.
Be ever active with His Spirit to carry and aid you.

Be the youthful son or daughter of the One.
Be earnest to share with all your love.
Go to the aid of all who are willing to travel in the way.

Rise up now. Be a strong wonder worker.
Great is the power and might of the Spirit within you.
Save those you can from the sea of ignorant and foolish ways.

You have been given the Spirit so that you might share with those in need.
You have been given its knowledge and wisdom to share with those who are
seeking the way.

With the approval of the One give eyes again to the blind.
Be like the ancient one; deliver those you meet from affliction.
Be like the ancient one; teach to and heal all those you meet.

Bestowed upon you is the Holy Spirit sent to you by the One.
Be a worthy vessel of a thousand treasures.

As you are now you are nobly born.
You are a son or daughter of the One.
Be a helper to all who call upon you with their troubles.
Accept your great responsibility.

Go to all who are in need with love.
Go to them with the fresh vigor of the Spirit.
Bear well the yoke and the obligations of being a Child.

# That I May Live

That I may live, I call unto the One.
I pray for the Spirit to be bestowed on me.
I pray for the precious treasures and gifts of the Spirit.
I pray that I will always be obedient to my calling.

Even as I am, I send forth my prayer to the One.
Even as I am, I ask to return to the journey to my true home.
Even as I am, I ask for the helpers to guide me on my way.
May the One find me worthy to come together with Him again.

Man strives with man for glory.
They are always eager to fight for their own glory.
May the One look upon me with favor.
May the One remove me from this vain way of life.

I have struggled and fought in many foolish ways.
I have been yoked by my own ignorance.
I have traveled to a far distance from my true home.
I ask for the Holy Spirit to guide me to the proper way.

May the glorious yoke of love be placed upon me.
May I be directed to the proper goal.
May I be made worthy to receive the friendship and love of the One.
May I be guided back to the noble Sacred Way.

May I be saved from the tyranny of my foolish ways.
May I be removed from the pit of my ignorance.
May the One encompass me with the Spirit.
May the One refresh me and take away my foolishness.

May I meet with the teachers and sages who can guide me.
May I meet with a doer of marvels who will show me the way.
May I be brought back to life again.
May I do great deeds to honor the One who has saved me.

I always thought the One was at some far distant place.
I was forlorn because of the treachery of those who claimed to be His Priests.
The Light of the Spirit has shown me that the One is always near.
The One is here to give His help. In His Love He stands with me.

Now I honor the One.
His Spirit has brought me abundant joy.
Always I will live in His presence.
Always I will speak His words to you.

The One provided me with the Spirit.
The Spirit has filled me with love, knowledge, and wisdom.
These I am to use to help all mortal men.

# What May We Do

What may we do to win God's grace?
What may we do that is pleasing to Him?
How can we, who are ignorant, worship Him?

Let those who are ignorant ask these questions of you.
You know the proper way to walk the noble path.
You know the path that is not for a spiritless mortal man.

Such a person as you, is all-wise.
We call upon you this day to declare the accepted prayer.
We call upon you with the love and honor due to such as you.

Simplify for us the ways of the Mighty One.
Share with us the wondrous teachings of the mystic word.
Save us from our foolish and ignorant ways.

Become to us a wise minister.
Teach us the words and hymns of the One.
Teach us to worship the One as is proper for His sons and daughters.

May the One turn His eyes to us.
May He send us the proper teacher of the Way.
May He accept our prayer and hymns of praise.

May our Teachers, Priests, and Sages guard us well.
May they keep us in safety from those who follow wicked ways.
May they bring to us the proper knowledge and wisdom.

Give us not up to the wicked man.
Keep us from straying far from the Sacred Way.
Keep us safe as we find our way home.

May those who love the One gain for you their friends.
Prepare for us the proper nourishment of knowledge.
Prepare to teach us the wisdom of the Sacred Way.

Show us how to obtain the Holy Spirit to lead us on the Holy Path.
Help us to find the contentment of the Sacred Way.

May what you teach hold me to the Sacred Way.
May this knowledge and wisdom be passed from man to man.
May the Spirit never depart from us.

Do not let us slumber in contempt of the Holy Life.
Do not let us falter and deviate from the Sacred Way.
Do not let us vanish and become lost to the Way.

# When Will the Guardians Awaken

When will the Guardians awaken to the plight of the Children of the One?
When will they again teach the Sacred Way?
When will they again follow the Holy Law of the One?

The One established the heavens and the earth.
The One pours forth the Holy Spirit to be a skillful worker.
The One is self-born, and He alone is worthy of our worship.

Daily the One is with us and observes our foolishness.
Daily the One is with us and hears our prayer.
Daily the One is with us to see if any will walk in His Way.

In joy He would restore us to the Sacred Way.
In joy He would restore us to the rite of proper worship.
In joy He would open wide the doors that cause men trouble.

As a wise parent, He has provided us with knowledge.
As a wise parent, He has stored for us great treasure.
As a wise parent, He has sought to guide our steps.

Here we have been born to learn the Sacred Way.
Here we have been born to experience many wonders.
Here we have been born to receive the Holy Spirit.

Those who should be our guides have treated us like cattle.
Those who should be our guides have kept us in fear.
Those who should be our guides have bound us with foolish ways.

It is time for mankind to awaken from its slumber.
It is time for mankind to be strengthened by knowledge and wisdom.
It is time for mankind to experience the Splendor of the Way.

We pray that we will receive a skillful teacher.
We pray that we will receive a proper guardian and guide.
We pray that the Holy Spirit will encompass us.

May the veils, which cloud our minds, be removed.
May the veils, which cloud our hearts, be removed.
May the light of knowledge remove the darkness of our ignorant ways.

Let us find our joy in the One who established the heavens and the earth.
Let us find our joy in establishing our relationship to the One.
Let us find our joy in following the Sacred Way.

Be strong and stay on the Holy Path.
Be strong and help those who are seeking the Way.
Be strong and save those who are willing from the dark pit.

The One will save us from the affliction of foolishness.
The One will save us from the misery of ignorance.
The One will save us from our fear and loneliness.

The One is always loving.
The One is always kind and will not fail us.
The One is always with us as we walk in His Way.

# Bring Your Understanding

Bring your understanding of the Sacred Way to all who will listen.
Receive the Holy Spirit, and let it be your guide.
Praise the One who created the heavens and the earth.

Be strong and accept your vocation.
Day and night pray that you may be a proper guide.
Show forth the Holy Spirit by the way you live your life.

Cheer us with the workings of the Spirit.
Delight us by showing to us the Holy Way.
Challenge us with your knowledge and wisdom.
May the One vouchsafe to us this favor.

Come with the teachings that will brighten our lives.
Show us how to receive the Holy Spirit of the One.
Show us how to honor our Father and our Mother.

May the One be with you as you accomplish this task.
May the One assent to what you have to teach.
May the One guide you and us to the Sacred Way.

Come before us with your words and your prayer.
Let all men hear them in the halls of worship.
We will be kind and listen to the words you have from the One.

Let us honor you for the gifts that you bestow on us.
Let us honor you for bringing knowledge of the One.
Let the words you teach us be the words of the One.

Teach us to become Children of the One.
Teach us to live in the Sacred Way of Love.
Teach us that we may enjoy returning to our home with the One.

Do not be frustrated because the common folk hate you.
Let the righteous gain salvation by proper worship of the One.
Let those who turn their backs and their hearts to the One suffer and waste away.

Come to us and teach us of God's love.
Urge us onward to live in the Sacred Way.
Be undaunted in all encounters and continue on your way.

Come to the men who will listen.
Continue to follow your sacred calling regardless of what people say.
Speed to do the work given to you by the One.

Do your work with love, and you will receive vigor.
Do your work with love, and the Spirit will guide you.
Do your work with love, and you will be following the Sacred Way.

We will rejoice when you come to us with your love.
We will become brave when you guide us to the proper way.
The One will be present with us each day.

Teach us to live in a pious way.
Teach us to discern the truth of the way.
The One will be with us to hear our words and prayer.

Show us the Way of the Spirit.
Show us the Way of Love.
Show us to the Sacred Way.

# The Holy Spirit

The Holy Spirit has been harnessed.
It has been harnessed for the immortal children so they may ascend.
They are to bring the light of knowledge and wisdom to the homes of men.
They are to be noble and active children in raising mankind from darkness.

The Holy Spirit was before all the living world was awakened.
She was the first created by the One.
She brings great treasure to those who win her care.

It is this Spirit that brings fortune this day to all the race of mortals.
She declares to the One God, our Savior and Friend, what she has seen each day.
May She declare that she found welcome in our home.
May She declare before the One that we were sinless today.

Each day the Spirit shows itself when it passes by.
The Spirit spreads the light of knowledge and wisdom each day.
The Spirit visits each dwelling to see if we are eager to learn.
To receive Her is the best of the goodly treasures, bestowed by the One.

Let all the brothers and sisters sing forth with joy.
Let us praise God for the strength He has bestowed.
Those who are intent to work evil will not grow in strength.
Each day they will be weakened till they are subdued.

Let our hymns be of the gladness we feel.
Let our thoughts be of joy to the One.
Let the flame of the Spirit shine forth through us.
May we show our lovely treasure to those who are still walking in dark and foolish ways.

When the light of the Spirit comes in, the darkness of ignorance forever departs.
Each day we grow in the brightness of knowledge and wisdom.
Our parents will forever surround us.
All gloom will depart.

The Spirit is the same in form today as when first created.
The Spirit will be the same tomorrow too.
It will guide us with the eternal statutes.
It will teach us to lead a blameless life.

The Spirit has the knowledge of the first beginning.
The Spirit and all of creation have been born out of the deep darkness.
The Spirit will not break the law of Order.
Day by day she will follow the appointed way.

The Spirit goes forth to see if any are willing.
She sees if any are willing to walk in the Sacred Way.
Ever youthful and smiling are those she finds worthy.
They wake up each day to discover the Spirit is within.

When you have the Spirit those who are seeking will see.
To them your form will be changed.
They will know you are one who follows the Sacred Way.
You will be blessed when you can guide and teach them of the Way.
Those who are not ready will think only that you are strange.

When you have the Spirit you will be rich in all the goodly treasures.
You will be continually working under the guidance and care of the One.
Never will the Spirit depart from you as long as you stay willing.
As long as you are willing, a happy fortune will be yours.

Always when you have the Spirit you will remain obedient to the reins of Law Eternal.
Each day you will be guided and given the appropriate thoughts.
Each day you remain with the Spirit will bring you greater blessing.

When you shine forth with the Spirit many will be swift to listen to your words and thoughts each day.

With you will be the richness of knowledge and wisdom.
You will lead many to the worship of the One.

# Each Day the Fire

Each day the fire of the Spirit is kindled in your heart and mind.
Each day you will shine with its brightness for all to see.
The Savior, our God, will send you forth to labor.
You will be active each day with labors of love.

You will meet individuals from many different generations.
You will interpret the Holy ordinances so that each may understand.
For endless mornings and days you will go forth in your labors of love.
The Spirit will work through you as long as you are willing.

Each day you will teach all you meet by the way you do your labors.
You will become an example for others to follow.
Truly they will see that you follow the Path of Order.
They will see that you do not fail in your labor of love.
They will see you know the Holy ordinances well.

Near the Spirit is seen, when you do your labors with love.
You show to others the sweet things that you have inside.
The Spirit you demonstrate will awaken many from their sleep.
Many will be led to return to the true and constant way.

Wider and wider will the circle grow as you labor with love.
The influence of the Spirit will be seen in an ever-growing circle.
Because of you many will experience the touch of love.
Many will return to the laps of their parents.

The effect of the Spirit is exceedingly vast.
Her light will be seen by kin and strangers alike.
She will not turn away from the high or the humble.
With the labors of your love all will feel the presence of the Spirit.

The Spirit seeks out men and women to see if they are willing.
To those who are willing she will come to them like a loving wife or husband.
She will unmask her beauty to all who are willing.
She will smile on them and give them knowledge and wisdom.

The Spirit will not leave the Way that is her place.
She will depart from those who will not follow the Way.
She will depart from those who are set in their foolish ways.
You must be willing or the Spirit will depart.

When the Spirit departs she takes with her love, knowledge, and wisdom.
She will vanish from those who turn to evil ways.
She will be like a shadowy memory until you return to the Way.

You may sleep on, unawakened. That is for you to choose.
For the One to send to you His Spirit you must be willing.
You may sleep on and waste your life away. That is for you to choose.

The Spirit of the One is available now to us.
She has encircled us with love.
She has come into each of our dwellings.
Will you accept her love and the yoke of the One?
Will you invite the Spirit to remain in your home?

The One will give you rest from troubles and strife.
When His Spirit remains in your home it will bring in an abundance of good.
You will be encircled by His love in all that you do.

The One loves us as His own Children.
He will bestow on us an abundance of knowledge and wisdom.
You may remain encircled by love and good favor.
You must however be willing to share this love.

# The Prudent One

The prudent one will rise early in the morning.
He will receive and entertain the Spirit of the One.
He will receive instruction and be directed throughout the day.
He will increase his life with proper activity.

The One will bestow great vital power to the prudent one.
He will bestow His treasure of knowledge and wisdom.
He will bestow all we need for our sustenance when we come to Him early
each day.

Each day the One comes to see if we are still willing.
Each day He comes to the sons and daughters of the Sacred Way.
Each day He gives us more from the Spirit and prospers us when we lead a
pious life.

He will bring to us the health-giving water of life.
As we come to Him with our love and worship, He will fill us full and prosper
us.
He will know when we are willing to serve and give freely of our love.

Everywhere in the heavens and upon the earth those who know exalt the One.
He is the liberal giver, whom all strive to know.
The water of life and all abundance originate with Him.

To those who give Him all their love, He gives immortality.
To those who provide loving service, He shows His splendor.
The One will lengthen the lifetime of these and be with them all their days.

Those who remain pious, He will not let sink to sin and sorrow.
He will be with them every day for their protection.
He will not let them suffer decay or affliction.

# With the Wisdom

With the Wisdom I have been given I present these words to you.
These lively praises of the One are given for all who are seeking.
With great simplicity they are written that all may understand.

The One, the unconquered King, our Father, has furnished me with more than
a thousand sacred teachings to be written.

I have accepted a great responsibility.
I pray that I will be permitted to complete this task.
For the glory of the One I will accomplish this work of love.

Beside me to guide me is the One God of all.
Within me is the Spirit, which causes all my words to flow.
They have one purpose; to draw all who read them to return to the Sacred
Way of the One.

A thousand different teachings are to lead us in the long journey to our
Father's side.
Some will read these writings with joy.
Some will read these writings and say this cannot be.

Many times in our history, these writings have been placed in the hands of
men.
Many times we have been given this great gift in many different forms.
Still mankind has seen fit to turn its back to the words given to us by the One.
Our Father waits for us to return to the Way.

# The One

The One has by His Holy Law anointed His Priests.
The Priests have been born to be most skilled for the Holy Work.
They have intense yearning to do the One's Holy work.

The Holy Priests are never deceived.
They receive guidance from the One to whom they pray.
With Love they sit in worship in the presence of the One.

They walk in the Sacred Path.
With reverence and love they perfect their worship.
All their ways and offerings are controlled by their love.

The Priests have become skilled in the presentation of knowledge and wisdom.
Their teachings have grown from the ancient way.
They have brought to mankind the knowledge that the One God is not far away.

In an ordered way, they have taught that the One traverses the earth and is always near.

The teachings of the One have been planted as seeds.
As mankind's abilities grow, the ideas planted as seeds will flower and bear fruits.

Each day the eyes of the One are upon us.
Each day He sees all that is happening upon the earth.
Each day He knows those who will work in the Holy Way.

The wise High Priests in every house take thought of the Sacred Way.
They take thought of how to accomplish the Holy Work.
They use all their mental power to lead others to the Sacred Way.

The One has instructed the Priests to do all in their power to guide and train those who strive to walk in His way.

There are to be no secrets kept from the seekers of the Way.
All who are seeking are to be treated as honored guests by those ordained as Priests of the Way.

The One will bestow His Spirit to all who are ready to accept its power.
To those who will be active in leading others to the Way the Spirit is given.

The One will accelerate the gift of the Spirit to those who are ready.
He will bestow a greater abundance of knowledge and wisdom.
He shall rescue us from the overwhelming suffering and misery which man is causing to man.

The One is the vast, universal Good.
He has and will continue to send us His messengers.
He has not and will not loosen His hold because of His love for mankind as a whole.

The Priests will continually seek to serve the One and mankind through acts of love.
The One bestows His blessings on each pious person.
He opens wide the doors of knowledge and wisdom for them.

The Priests are to be the most kind of mankind.
They are to walk in the Sacred Way of Love and be like the One.
They are to teach mankind the sacred rite.

All their worship and their prayers are to the One God alone.

With the wisdom and knowledge the Priests have been granted they are to serve in the work of the One.

They are most dear to Him.
They are to be most thoughtful of the plight of mankind.
They are to be messengers of truth and love to them.

144

The One God, despite our extreme foolishness, loves mankind.
The One knows all we think and do.
He has sent us Priests, Teachers, and Sages to lead us out of our ignorant ways.

The One is our dear Father and Friend.
When we will but turn to Him—He will come to our aid.
When we but ask for His help—He will come to our aid.
He would have us return to the Ancient Sacred Way.

# The Spirit of the One

The Spirit of the One is given to individuals who enter into His service.
Mankind may think it is far away, but it is always near.
The Blameless ones receive it in great abundance.

Swiftly it comes to us for our help.
It will be strong in those who have prepared their heart and mind.
Those who receive the Spirit will become blameless and active.

The One does hear the prayer and words of all mankind.
Mankind goes to Him for strength in every fight.
Mankind goes to Him for victory in every war.

He knows who the true heroes are.
Those who seek the good of mankind and to serve God with love receive His aid.
They receive of His Spirit to guide and improve the state of man.

The Mighty One hides the Spirit from the wicked man.
He keeps it far away from those who are out for their own gain.
When man seeks to glorify himself he is cut off from any divine aid.

We wish that the One will look upon us with favor.
We wish that the One will be our dear Friend.
We wish that the One will be our strong ally.

He aids those who serve Him with love.
He aids those who serve mankind with love.
With His aid there is no enemy to cast down.

Rid yourselves of overwhelming Pride.
Consume it in the flame of the Holy Spirit.
Serve with all your might the ancient Holy One.

As a Priest of the One, drive all the sins of man away.
As a Priest of the One, guide mankind, as was done by the heroes of old.
As a Priest of the One, seek out with love those who have lost their way.

With the presence of the Holy Spirit a Priest has great power.
He or She may invoke the aid of the One.
He or She may call upon the love of the One to protect and heal.
He or She may call upon the One and awaken the power of the demon-slaying prayer.

The Priests of the One have within their power the ability to drive death far away.
The Priest of the One have within their power the ability to drive from us all hate.
Those who speak and do wickedness will flee from the Priest of the One and vanish like a mote of dust.

By thoughtful prayer we may obtain the great wealth of wisdom and knowledge.
By thoughtful prayer we may become sons and daughters of the One.

The One is waiting for us to commit to the Sacred Way.
The One will know when our call to Him is inspired and true.
The One will know when our heart and mind is filled with love.

For your good and ours, come to the One God.
Ask His aid to end your foolish and ignorant way.
Ask His aid to drive all wickedness away.
Ask His aid to overcome the evil-hearted ones with love.

If we truly walk in the Sacred Way no weapon may harm us.
The evil-hearted destroy themselves and may not harm us.
The Spirit of the One encircles us and protects us with love.

May the One come to us with a rich abundance of knowledge and wisdom.
May the One come to us and lead us by an unobstructed path.
May the One be with us so we will not stray from the Way.

May the One guide us and welcome us home.
May the One always protect us as we strive to find our way.

There is only One God.
There is one source of knowledge and wisdom.
There is one that is strong enough to give us aid.
There is one Savior, the Immortal One, to help us.
There is only One who can keep us from all harm.

There is only One who we are to love and worship.
There is only One who is the Lord and God of all mankind.
There is only One who can remove the veils of our ignorance.
There is only One who is the Good, the Father of all mankind.

# Come to Us

Come to us Lord Most High, wherever you are.
Come and show us the way to our ancient home.
Gather us within your arms, and guide us please.

We invoke you to come to us.
We offer to you our most precious gifts; our hearts and minds.
Be to us a Father and treat us as your children.

God, our Father, encircle us with your Holy Spirit.
Let us drink from your spring the water of life.
Quench our thirst to know the ancient Sacred Way.

Refresh us with your strength.
Share with us the sweetness that should be in our life.
Come and be with us each and every day.

Guide us to find the treasure of your knowledge and wisdom.
Do not let it remain concealed and hidden.
Remove from us the stone we call our heart and replace it with one filled with
your love.

Let us strive with all our might to win your favor.
Reveal to us how to win the Spirit, which has been concealed.
Guide us and open the doors within our hearts and minds.

Grasp us with both hands and shake us till we awaken.
Most High God, awaken us and put an end to our foolish ways.
You are the Lord of majesty and strength.
Guide us with your Lordly might.

Father, we know that you could crush down the veils that blind our eyes.
We know that you could flood us with more than we could bear.
We know that with your strength you control all that we receive.

Little by little you have revealed to us your mighty strength.
You have taught us to search and learn in the proper way.
Let us be joined now with your strength for all eternity.

You have provided for all of the needs of mankind.
You have poured forth your Spirit to all of mankind.
May we have the wisdom to use your Spirit in the proper way.

Mankind is eager to obtain riches.
Mankind is eager to be craftsmen of leisure.
Mankind has missed the happiness that only comes from the journey of life.
Mankind has forgotten the bliss received in the Sacred Way.

Mankind has sought to do great deeds of might.
Mankind has sought to win at any cost, a life of leisure.
Mankind has missed the ultimate prize of eternal life.
You, O Lord, have hidden the prize away.

Most High God, do not forsake your worshipers now.
Be at hand to help us as we try to make our way.
Guide us to the proper way with the light only you can bestow.

We are plagued with the lawless, who are only interested in self-gain.
We are surrounded by those who have turned their backs to the Holy Laws.
We are surrounded by those who have turned their backs to the Sacred Way.
Many seem set on tyrannizing those who are seeking to follow the Sacred Way.

Lord of Power, make us strong that we will follow the way.
Lord of Power, give us the proper words to say to those who would block our way.
Lord of Power, prevent us from being turned from the Sacred Way.

Many would have us think, O Lord, that you are too far away.
Many would have us believe that there is no hope of help from you.

Many would have us turn from you with the promise of happiness if we come
with them on their way.

Many are the promises of wealth and fame if we turn from the Way.
Many are the promises of luxury and an easy life if we turn from the Way.
Many are the promises of those who are blind to the Sacred Way.

Help us now, O Lord, with your strength.
Save us from being turned from the Sacred Way.
We look to you for our happiness.
We look to you for knowledge and wisdom.
We look to you to be our guide.
We look to you to be with us day by day.

Encircle us with your love.
Encircle us with your care.
Encircle us with the Holy Spirit.
Keep us within your arms as your child.
Keep us on the Sacred Way.

# In the Days of Old

In the days of old we subdued men who disagreed with us by fighting in bloody wars.
Each side claimed to have their God as their helper.
Each side claimed to be guided by the Spirit of God.
The winner of the war divided their spoil with their Priests.
Such was said to be the will of their God.

In war no one wins the approval of the One God.
No one receives the light of knowledge and wisdom.
Wars are fought to satisfy the lusts and for the vainglory of ignorant men.
The One God has no part in the wars of foolish and ignorant men.

The One waits for mankind to come to Him with the free offerings of our hearts and minds.

The One waits for mankind to come to Him with their love.
Waiting for us are His bounteous gifts, the good gifts of the One who is the Good.

As in days of old we must choose to follow the Sacred Way.
We must choose how we will live in this place called the earth.
We must choose to make the place we are a sacred place, wherever that may be.

Speak now to us and make the truth known to us.
This we ask of the One and of all who have received the beams of light of His knowledge and wisdom.

The One God is indeed to be found by the true seekers of the Sacred Way.

It is a great deed to be lauded, as in the days of old for an individual to commit to follow in the Sacred Way.

With commitment the doors of the mind and heart are opened.
With commitment we are given aid in our quest.

To those who commit and follow the Holy Law, the Holy Spirit is given.
They are then worthy to be called true heroes and guides.
They are then worthy of our respect, honor, and love.

It is the wise plan of the One that these true heroes lead the people forth in their journey.

They do not seek fame and glory in the battles of men.
They seek to glorify the One God in the lives of men.

In times of need they lead the people to the One who gives life to all.
In times of need they lead the people to the One who is the only true place of rest.

They demonstrate to the people that the One will welcome them as they begin the Sacred Journey.

With the One guiding them, those committed to the Way will become the true champions of the people.

They will become our Teachers, Sages, and Priests.
They will be instrumental in guiding us to the Sacred Path.
They will be instrumental in guiding us in our journey through life.
They will help us to return to our ancient home.

# Living in the Sacred Way

Living is the Sacred Way we are purged of our former foolishness.
Both the heavens and the earth will come to aid us.
The One God will guide us in the proper way.

Mankind will be divided into those who serve the One and those who have not yet entered the Way.

Some will say it will lead to the conflict between the Sons of God and the Sons of man.

Some will say the Sons of God are destined for heaven and the sons of man are destined for the pit.

Living in the Sacred Way we will learn the secret of what many have called the Sorcerer's Stone.

We will learn that there is no deep and narrow pit reserved for the wayward man.

Living in the Sacred Way we will learn the true brotherhood of all mankind.
We will learn to lovingly guide the wayward man back to the Holy Way.
We will learn that the love of the One extends to all mankind.

We are not to seek to destroy those who have differing ways.
We are not to count men, great or small, based on how they choose to worship.

We are to provide loving guidance to all who seek the Sacred Way.
We are to do good deeds for all who are in need.

The One God could have chosen to crush all of mankind for many different reasons.
The One God did not choose to terminate mankind because of our continued foolish and ignorant ways.

He has patiently waited for us to turn to Him with love.
He has protected us from extinction because of His love.

Many have declared themselves to be the mighty ones of God.
Many have sought to keep mankind living in fear.

The One God will put these people in their place.
The One God will shake them until they are in great fear.
The One God will not slay those who have demonstrated their foolishness but will let them live with their fears.

Only ignorant men seek to slay other men in the name of their God.

Living in the Sacred Way we gain the gift of the Holy Spirit.
We gain the wealth of knowledge and wisdom from the One.
We gain the knowledge that a loving God, who is the Father of all mankind, does not originate hostilities.

We learn that those who engage in hostilities will not go unchecked by the One.
We learn that lasting wealth and success will only come as the result of serving the One and mankind with our love.

# Come Speedily

Come speedily to the feast that has been prepared by the One.
A feast is prepared for all who journey on the way home.
The Holy Spirit is prepared for all when they have prepared.

Discern well and uplift your mind to the One.
Be glad in your words and hymns and gratify your mind.
Come to receive the gift of the Holy Spirit of the One.

The receipt of the Holy Spirit will give you joy.
It will gladden you in all the tasks that you do.
It will make your work for mankind most effective.
Come to the One well prepared and give Him your love.

The Holy Spirit will be a great aid.
You will learn, step by step, to skillfully use its power.
Many may want to come and be associated with you because the One seems
to grant all your prayers.

They will be tempted to address their hymns and prayers to you instead of the
One.

With the Holy Spirit to guide you, you will be most able to make wishes of the
people come true.

With the Holy Spirit to guide you, you will be able to draw people out of their
slumber.

Wake up those who are willing.
Wake up the intelligence of their mind.
Wake up the love that is hidden in their heart.

Illuminate the sacred teachings from the heavens and the earth.
Illuminate your heart and mind for the glory of the One.

Put on the robe of the Holy Spirit.
Display its radiance so that all may awaken.
Awaken mankind from the womb of death into the radiance of eternal life.

Through you the Holy Spirit will quickly flow to all who are in need.
Strong will be your power to heighten the awareness of their hearts and minds.
Through the example you set they, too, may want to receive the Holy Spirit to be a guide in their life.

Those who do not wish to be awakened will be like cowards and may speedily turn away.

With the One at your side, with the Holy Spirit working through you, you will be protected in all that you do.

You will be protected in every part of the world.

When you have properly prepared and learned to use the Spirit, you will become like a first-born son of the One.

At your disposal will be the full knowledge and wisdom of the One.
You will have full power to free individuals and remove from them the taint of sin.

For you the Holy Spirit will go to all who have your love.
It will yield amazing results that many may consider to be miracles.
You will know it is the natural workings and results of the Spirit of the One.

# The Sacred Way

The Sacred Way has been prepared for you.
Come by yourself or come with a hundred or a thousand friends.
The Holy Spirit, the divine gift from the One, is waiting for you.
Come and be one of the first to receive it in our generation.

The Holy Spirit is waiting to bring to you the joy of the Holy life.
The Holy Spirit is waiting to give you strength.

Come and be purified by the Spirit of the One.
Accept it as your robe for life.
Accept the splendor of its power.
Clothe yourself with the light of knowledge and wisdom.

For you the Holy Spirit is waiting.
It will come to you with your full portion of the Good.
It will come to you and make you a leader of men if you are willing.
Come to the One with your love.
Come to the One, well inclined to do loving service for man.

Come alone; come with a hundred or a thousand friends.
Come and partake in the Holy rite.
Come to taste the sacred food provided by the One.
Come to the One with love.
Come to the One with an open heart and mind.

The Spirit is waiting to make you a radiant child of the One.
Accept the Holy Spirit that is offered to you by the chosen Priests of the One.

The One will greet you if you will come to Him.
He will be with you to guard you from all harm.

He will be with you to give you the sacred food.
He will be with you to bestow upon you the Holy Spirit.

He is waiting for you to choose.
He is waiting for you to accept your place in His Way.
He is waiting for you to commit to living in a Sacred Way.
Your bounty as his child will be waiting for you when you return to Him with your love.

May our words and our songs bring you to the solemn Holy Rite of the One.
May you come and become a vigorous worker for the One.
May you come and be well inclined to do loving service for the good of all mankind.
May you come and help us to spread the Holy word.

Come now and accept your portion of the work to bring others into the Sacred Way.
Come now with your love to do the work of the One.
Come and be gladdened that you have returned to the Way.

The Holy Spirit and the Waters of Life are waiting for you.
They have been offered to you by the Chosen Priests of the One.
They are offered up to you if you will walk in the Way.
Your Father is waiting to welcome you for the journey home.

Much work is needed to awaken all of mankind from its slumber.
It may be necessary to take with you the Spirit and go house to house.
It may be necessary to go within each dwelling.
To awaken mankind from its slumber is no easy task.

Come now if you are willing.
Commit to loving service for your Father, the One.
Commit to the task of awakening mankind from its deep slumber.

The One is waiting for you.
He is waiting to bestow on you the Holy Spirit.
He is waiting for you to accept His love.
He is waiting for you to commit to the Sacred Way.

# Bring the Offering

Bring the offering of your love to the One.
Bring to Him your most excellent hymns of praise.
Bring to Him your words, thoughts, and deeds.

He is the bountiful and loving Father of all mankind.
He is most pleased when we walk in the Sacred Way.
With His aid, those with wicked ways will never harm us.

The One has set a wide path for all who love Him to walk therein.
His Spirit has maintained the Path of Holy Law.
It is there for us even in this day.

Firm-set is the way to our Father's home.
Firm-set are the laws, which we must follow.
The Holy Spirit will aid us in our journey.
It will give us a great strength, which merits praise.
It will give us a great power to overcome all that does not enhance the Sacred
Life.

The One will uphold us with the Holy Spirit.
He will uphold all who walk in the Way.
He will come and be with us day by day.

The One is a giver of liberal gifts to all His children.
He is the great One, the Mover of all men.

The Holy Spirit is most sweet and loving to all who come to the One.
All who come will have their share of its bounty.
May all who will, come and accept the Spirit today.
May all who will, come and work with one accord in Love of the One.

Come and accept the joyfulness of the Spirit.
Become a righteous one who walks in the Sacred Way.
With the aid of the Holy Spirit you may accomplish whatever is asked of you as you walk in the Way.

Whoever with their worship serves the One God, will receive His protection.
His Holy Spirit will guard you most carefully.
His Holy Spirit will keep you uninjured and free from distress.

The Spirit guards all the children well who act uprightly following the Law of the One.

The One beautifies the services with His presence when He is the object of our love and praise.

In all my worship I will profess the One is our Father.
He is the creator of all the heavens and the earth.
He is a bounteous giver to all His children.
He is the Compassionate One who is worthy of our praise.

Long may we live and perform loving service when we have His Spirit's help.

With the One God's help, with His Spirit ever guiding our way, we may be held to be His children.

He will be our shelter, our provider, and our wealth.

# When Our Hearts and Minds

When our hearts and minds have been prepared the Spirit comes.
The Holy Spirit comes to us when we are ready.
The Spirit brings with it knowledge and wisdom to nourish us.

Come to us now. Come and nourish us with knowledge and wisdom.
The Spirit will come to us and gladden us and correct the error of our ways.

Receive now the Holy Spirit.
Let it be expressed through you.
Let it awaken the sleeping powers within.
Awaken now to the power symbolized by the Sun's rays.

Take now the Holy Spirit within to enlighten you.
The Spirit is waiting to guide you upon the Sacred Way.

The Holy Spirit is all around you.
It waits to feed you till you are willing.
It will not overpower you or force upon you its power.

It is a gift from our loving Father.
It is a gift, which He asks us to accept.

# From the Most Ancient of Days

From the most ancient of days, the power of the Spirit has been known.
The glory of the Spirit's might is never faint.

Seeking communion with the One, I call the Spirit to help.
I ask the Spirit to lead me to the source of all bliss.

What has the power to draw to the One the hearts of all mankind?
Is it not the Holy Spirit—the active power of the One.

With the receipt of the Holy Spirit we are moved swiftly upon our way.
With the Holy Spirit aiding us, all our foes do flee.

As a man I call to the One God, the giver of bliss.
I call upon the One God to be my friend.

Many sing of the joyful friendship of God.
Some speak of the advantages enjoyed with the One's friendship.

A few speak of the grace of God with wisdom because they have first-hand
experience.

A few advanced in wisdom no longer speak but work to demonstrate to others
by the Way they Live.

In the recent course of time many pray for monetary wealth.
Few pray for the wealth of knowledge and wisdom.

In the recent course of time many speak of stirring the One to anger.
Few speak about the love of the One for all mankind.

Many ask the One to not become full of anger.
Many ask the One to come to us with His free gifts.
Many offer the One goats and sheep in return.

The wonder worker, the One God, is not to be bought with bribes and sacrifices of innocent lives.

The One is not concerned with our desire for fame.

The One is concerned that we come with open minds.
The One is concerned that we come with open hearts.
Most of all, the One, desires that we come to Him with our love.
Without love, all our words, songs, and prayers are vain.

Do not make vain promises, then try to slight the One.
Do not ask for His Spirit, then refuse to walk in the Sacred Path.

No harm is done to the One, but to yourself great harm is done.

If you wish the friendship of the One, be a friend to all mankind.
Be a whole-hearted friend to those who are in need.

Be a friend to all you meet,
Then the One may find you worthy of His friendship too.

# Our Prayers Are Heard

Our prayers are heard.
If in thought we honor the One—He hears our prayers.
If we walk in the Sacred Way—He hears our prayers.
When our latest thought is raised in love—He hears.
When we are centered well in love—He hears.

Our songs, Our words, Our very thoughts when sent out with love are in His presence immediately.

Many cannot accept these simple thoughts.
Many have taken to themselves the untrue above the true.
With minds fixed on the untrue, we rob ourselves of wisdom's mental energy.

Have you met, where you sit or dwell, the One of whom we speak?
I speak not of meeting just in your thoughts or mind.
I speak not of meeting just in an extreme Spiritual state.
Have you seen the One with your eyes, with the eyes the Holy Spirit gives?

The pious call to the One with loving hymns of praise.
These living men call to the One with their love of mankind.
All glory is given to the One by them for the deeds they do.
All nourishment and the wealth of knowledge and wisdom comes from the One to them.

Well it is known that all depends on the One.
It is He who opens the doorways of the heart and mind.
It is He who places upon us His yoke of love.

Without the One all our rites are meaningless.
Without the One we have no power to walk in the Sacred Way.

Without the One we will not find the right path.
Without the One we will not find the direct path to our home.

We pray to the One to give us strength.
We pray for His great power to keep us safe.
We pray we will receive His blessing day and night.

The offering, which we bring to the One, is our love.
With our love our prayers never fail.

The gifts of the One are only given to those who come to Him with their love.
The gifts He does bestow never fail when we remain with Him in love.

The Holy Spirit is the gift of the Strong One, our God.
It is given to the true heroes of mankind.
It is given to those who serve mankind with love.

Quickly now, come and hear our words.
Seek out and find those who speak of God and His love.
Seek out and find those who are led by His Spirit.

Receive knowledge from the one who knows God's Spirit well.
Join with them in the Holy work of love for the One.
Receive as they have, the Holy Spirit of the One.
Learn to know her well.

Never will the doing of loving service grow old.
Never will the doing of loving deeds fall into decay.
Never will the One withdraw His love from the righteous man.

God's love is renewed in every age.
God's love is renewed in every generation.
God's love is renewed each and every day.
God's love surpasses the highest concepts of mortal man.

Many would have us believe that God's love is hard to gain.
Many would have us believe that God's love is too different for mortal man
to understand or achieve.

Many would have us believe that only they know the way to receive His love.

Nothing could be further from the truth.

Since the most ancient of days, mankind's teachers have known.
The One God knows each of us since the time of our birth.

The One God is connected with each of us at birth.
Those of High Station know this connection can never be broken.
Always is the One with us waiting for us to accept His love.

Let the invokers bless, and they will receive His love.
Let those who bring offering bring them in love, and they will receive His love.
They will receive the choicest gift, the Holy Spirit of the One.
Let those who bring their friendship come, and they will receive the most excellent friendship in return.

With your ears, let them hear the still small voice of the One.
With your eyes, let them see the One is ever at your side.
The One brings to all who love the waters of life.
The One gives to all who love a true resting place.

The One God is not in some far off heaven.
The One God has made the earth His dwelling place.
The One God has made your home, His home.

He is ever at your side when you accept His love.
He is ever at your side when you follow the Sacred Way.
He is ever at your side to give you drink from the waters of life.

Will you accept this One God and give Him your love?

# The One God

The One God is not seated upon altars built by man.
The One God resides within the loving hearts of mankind.
Loving well this home of His, He brings to those in whom He dwells His food
of love as if we were His birthplace.

The Loving One bestows on those in whom He dwells the robe of His Holy
Spirit.
He clothes them with His love.

The lovers of God are like a child of a double birth.
They have been born of water from the womb of the earth.
They have been born of the Spirit of the One.

Each day they grow anew.
Each day they grow in physical, mental, and spiritual power.

The pair, the earth and the spirit, dwell together in these children of a double
birth.
Both parents hasten to the child with their care.
We may not comprehend the working of our parents, but they are there with
their care and love.

Ever will they be watchful and cherish the one who is their child.
How unfortunate it has been for mankind that many have tried to destroy this
bond of love.

Impetuous-tongued men have led many away from the understanding of this
bond.
They have done a great disservice to man.

Many have blackened the minds of men with false teachings.
They would have you love only the Spirit and reject your mother.
They would have you love only the Earth and reject the Spirit.

Their teachings bring discord to the minds of men.
They are impatient and would yoke you forever in darkness.
They will call their darkness the light of heaven.

The horror of a divided heart and mind follows in their way.
Gloom and despair is all they truly offer to mankind.
They will roar and claim you will incur God's anger if you do not follow them.
Such teachings have brought great sadness and despair to all mankind.

Going to great lengths, false teachers will do most anything to stop the development of mankind.
They will try to stop mankind from learning to honor both their Father and their Mother.

Their very survival depends on keeping from mankind the knowledge of our double birth.

Their very survival depends on there being no harmony on earth.

It has now been uncovered for you the meaning of our double-birth.
Let us grasp the meaning and display our understanding well.
Within each of us is the resting place of the One.

Let us awaken to the knowledge of mankind's double birth.
Let us bring back harmony and the love of our Father and Mother.
Let us learn to use their powers in harmony.
Let us gather within us our God-like power.
Let us blend together as true children of the One and honor both our Mother and our Father.

By honoring the two we rise up again to meet the Living One.
He will release us from the age of ignorance and end our foolish ways.
He will come again to make His dwelling within us.

The One will fill us with the Spirit of Harmony.
He will give us a new way of living.
We will be unsubdued in living in the Sacred Way of Love.

Our Mother will no longer be neglected and abused.
We will be able to wander in the fields and woods at peace with all the mighty beasts.
She will strengthen us again with the knowledge of Her ways.
She will strengthen us that we may properly use the power of the Spirit while maintaining harmony with all.

We are still like infants in our development.
Harmony with and honor of our Father and Mother will take us far.
We may even learn our place in this universe of ours.

May our prayer be for harmony and love.
May we leave behind discord and strife.
May the brilliance of truth shine in our form.
May we obtain the true knowledge and wisdom of the One.

Grant to be with us as our perfect Guide.
Grant to teach us in the proper Way.
Be with us and Guide us as we seek the Sacred Way.
This we ask of the One with all sincerity and love.

Welcome our prayer with your approval, God, Most High.
May your earth and your spirit work in harmony with us and teach us your ways.
May we properly learn and choose to be your children.
May we never deviate from the Sacred Way.

# The Very Existence of the One

The very existence of the One God has been forever established in the hearts
and minds of men.

He is the prime source of our strength.
Because of Him we strive to lead a Holy Life.

He is the Wonderful One.
He provides us with knowledge and wisdom.
He dwells upon the earth in the hearts of men.
He has provided us the Ten Principles by which all must live.

The One has given us a wonderful form.
All of us contain that which is immortal within our mortal frame.
He has the power to control each action but He lets us decide.
As in days of old, the One remains concealed till we choose.

From the Highest Father the Holy Spirit is brought to us.
He rises within us when we accept and believe in our double birth.
As we respond and join the two in harmony we learn to be as one.
Most youthful will we be and radiate the Spiritual Light for all to see.

Our Father through the Spirit joined with our Mother, the earth.
Humankind is their offspring, their child.
Those who believe this are increased in magnitude.
They are made pure and protected from all harm.

We have been given the freedom to choose the herald we will follow.
We have been given the freedom to choose the gifts that we will receive.
The One has the power to fully control us, but this is not His will.
He reserves the most sacred gifts for those who choose His Way.

What a time the Holy One has had with His Children.
They wander the world unrestrained on paths far from the Sacred Way.
They invent many gods who have no true power.
They turn their backs upon their pure birth to follow sundry paths.

There are those who have developed and know their art and have led many astray.
They have claimed to have visited the highest heaven.
They have lifted themselves aloft as the true guides of mankind.
They have no true strength, but bring much violence into the lives of men.

Still there are a few who guard and observe the Holy Law.
With the aid of the One they become very strong.
These few hold the keys to the spokes of the Holy Wheel.
They are pervaded by the Holy Spirit and are of the twice born.

All their teachings are ever presented to us in new forms.
They bring us back to the Lord of the House in the proper way.
They bring us the wealth of knowledge and wisdom that guides all worlds.
The very wise, with the assent of the One, lead us to our home on the Sacred Path of Love.

The One has vouchsafed to us that we will meet with a proper guide.
May he or she, a Chosen Priest, Sage, or Teacher, hear our call.
May we welcome them with joy and respond to their direction.
May they lead and guide us to our bliss and happiness.

The One is waiting for us to return by the Sacred Way.
The Universal Father is waiting for us to call forth His aid.
He is waiting to send us His Teachers, Sages, and Priests.
He is waiting to bestow the Holy Spirit upon those who choose His Way.

# Allow Your Hearts and Minds

Allow your hearts and minds to be kindled with love today.
Bring the love you have inside to the One God today.
Accept His gift, the gift of the Holy Spirit to be your guide.

In all your dealings be enriched by the Sacred Way of Love.
All your toils done with love bring glory to the One.
Working with love the Holy Spirit will be your guide.

The Wondrous One will sanctify all you do with love.
The Sacred Way has been firmly established for all who are seeking.
The Love of the One will encircle all who wish to return.

With the Wonderful One you have a Friend beyond compare.
His guidance will ring true in your heart and mind.
He waits for you to call upon His guidance and care.

The Holy Spirit will lead you to the well-ordered Sacred Way.
The One waits to receive you as His child when you return.
His many gifts will be waiting for you when you return.

Throw open the Divine Doors with your heart and mind.
The Love of the One will be unfailing when you perform this rite.
This rite is required and much desired, for the One will be active in your life.

Perform this rite in the night or in the day.
Be united again with your Father and your Mother.
Seat them together within your heart and mind so you may receive their guidance and love.

May you bring the two together in a harmonious way.
These sweet-voiced lovers will guide you each day.
Complete this and you will be on the Sacred Way.

Sit in harmony with your Father and your Mother.
Love will encircle you on all sides.
You will take your true place as a wonder worker for the One.

Abundant and wonderful are the gifts that they bestow.
For your increase and growth, wisdom and knowledge are their gifts.
You will become a true kinsman and a true friend to all.

Give forth your love and call to the One for guidance.
Ask to be led on the Sacred Way of Harmony and Love.
Accept the intelligence, which is within you today.

Be joined today with your Father and your Mother.
Let them inspire you to walk in the Sacred Way.
Accept from them the gift of their love.

Come now and enjoy the gift that is offered to you.
Come back to the One and accept the calling.
You are invited to walk as one on the Sacred Way.

# To All Who Will Listen

To all who will listen I present ancient teachings in a new way.
I bring my words forth for the glory of the One.
We are the offspring, the children, bearing most precious things.
In season we bring forth again the ancient teachings.

I will not claim to be All Wise.
I will not claim to have visited the Highest Heaven.
I will claim that my words are brought to you with my love.
I will claim that I am one of many children who love the One.

The flames of the Holy Spirit will not grow cold.
When you look upon the One the loveliness of His face will shine upon your
face for all with eyes to see.

The active force of the One is His Spirit, which brings to you the Light of
knowledge and wisdom.

This light never sleeps, and is ageless, and will change your life.

Send with your words and your hymns your love to the One.
You dwell within His abode.
He is the One Sovereign Lord.
Come with your love into your center, and find your home.

No force known to man could prevent the One from having His way.
Because of His love, He has allowed us the freedom to choose our own way.
Because of His love, He waits to welcome us when we return to our home.

He could grant us our wish for untold wealth.
He could come and smite all our foes.

He could come and direct our every step.
But this is not His way.

When we return of our own free will, He will be our aid.
He will find enjoyment in our praise.
He will grant our wish for the wealth of knowledge and wisdom.
He will be with our prayers to gain their desired end.
He will be with us to guide and aid us when we come to Him with our love.

The kindler of the Spirit within wins the One as a Friend.
The promoter of the Holy Law within wins the One as a guide.
The promoters of the Way of Love find their Father is the One.

The Children of the One are guarded on every side.
The Mighty One encircles them with His love.
He is the helper and guide to all who strive for the Sacred Way.
He will keep His children safe from harm.

# The Priests Go Forth

The Priests go forth in the Sacred Way.
With wondrous power the Holy Spirit guides them.
They will not turn to the right or the left.
They will do all that they do with love.

The Priests go forth to teach and uphold the Holy Law.
They are encompassed by love and seek to lead others on their journey to their
birthplace with the One.

With love they will use their god-like powers.

The Priests go forth to those who are seeking the Way.
They will guide all to reach the selfsame end.
The One must be duly invoked by us to become our guide.
They will guide us in the proper way to seek His aid.

The One observes the trends set in motion by man.
He observes all who seek to dwell together in harmony.
By day and by night He stands ready to make us young again.
He stands ready to accept us as His children when we call to Him.

The One will come in answer to our loving devotions.
He will animate us in ten ways when we call to Him.
He will be our helpmate and our guide.
New deeds will be performed each day for those who love Him.

The One will be like a shepherd to those who walk in His Way.
He will guide and protect them in every way.
He will love them and keep them in His care.

May the One find joy in our words and deeds.
May the One find joy in our prayer.
May the One sustain us as we seek the Holy Way.
May the One deliver to us the untainted Holy Law.
May the One always be with us and guide us home.

# Ask the One

Ask the One what you will.
He has come and is now at your side.
He knows the answers you seek.
He is full of wisdom and ready to be your guide.

With Him are admonitions.
With Him are commands.
He is the Lord of Strength.
He is the Lord of Power and Might.

Ask the One what you will.
Not all are willing to learn by their questioning.
Many will only follow the thoughts of their own mind.

Forget not the former words of the One.
Forget not the later words of the One.
Go forth and seek your answers.
Do not be careless, for none exceed the mental power of the One.

Always bring your questions to the One.
He will give ear to all the words you speak.
He will answer and speed you on the Sacred Way.
You are the babe. He considers His child.

You may not grasp all the answers, but keep going forward.
A little further on and straightaway you will understand.
You are newly born and guided in each step by your kin.

When the One stirs you to action you will find joy.
You will find pleasure and great gifts in the Sacred Way.
Always will you approach the One as His child.

Many will consider these wild teachings.
Many will turn their back on the One.
Many will declare these are words of a mere mortal.

The One has declared the lore of works to mortals.
The Wise One has declared to mortals His law.
The wise mortal will declare the truthful teachings he or she has received.

# Honor the Holy Spirit

Honor the Holy Spirit when it comes to you.
It is an all-perfect guide to those who awaken to its presence.
It is within all that moves and moves not.
The One has placed within and around us the Spirit to be our guide.

Do not be the fool who ignored the guidance of His parents.
Do not feel you can stand and remain untouched on your own.
Without the proper guide only a fool will attempt to walk on the lofty paths
upon this earth.

Take the Spirit to be your guide.

There are many paths going forth in all directions.
All in the end come together at the proper destination.
Each path has been carefully measured out for those who travel in that way.
Entrust your desires to the One, and you will be guided to your proper path.

The prudent Sages, Teachers, and Priests let the One lead them to His
dwelling.
They accept His love and care, and seek to serve the One.
They guard with their various skills the Law of the One.
It is to these men and women that the Spirit is most manifest.

All men and women in all regions have been of noble birth.
It is our aim that all men and women will awaken and see this.
All life, be it great or small, has been given to us by the One.

He is the Father of all.

We will one day awaken to the fact that we are all His children.
We will one day live in a way worthy of our noble birth.

# When Piercing the Veil

When piercing the veil of ignorance we often experience great friction.
We experience friction from those who cannot see.
We experience friction in the clash of the new with the old ways.
Let us not falter when we experience this friction.

The heralds of the One God come to us in many forms.
They have been set within the many human houses.
They have been sent to disperse to man the light of knowledge and wisdom.
Their teachings shine forth with beauty to our hearts and minds.

The heralds of the One God are not to be harmed.
They bring to us the knowledge and wisdom of the One.
They have the protection and the approval of God.
All their acts and words are guided by His love.

The One is seated in their hearts and is their constant focus.
The teachings of the One have been constant since the beginning.
Men and women skilled in worship have established them in the hearts and
minds of all races of mankind.

Guided by the Holy Spirit the heralds of the One have been here to instruct
and guide mankind.

The teachings of the One have contained many wondrous things.
They clarify or crush many things taught to us by man.
They drive away the darkness caused by ignorant man.
They shine forth like beacon lights in the multitude of forms established by
man.
Each day they shine anew in the hearts and minds of those who are awakening
from their slumber.

The new worshipers, while still like an embryo in their knowledge and skills, may experience hostility from those who have no understanding.

They may never be injured by these individuals with no understanding. Though men and women are blind and sightless they will not be harmed by the splendor of the One.

Those who are lovers of the One will preserve even those who are blind and wish to do them harm.

# Here upon the Earth

Here upon the earth the Lord our God has hastened to place for us a great treasure.

The Holy Spirit serves Him to bring us near to Him.

The Holy Spirit steers the inhabitants of the heavens and the earth by the glory of the One.

It is the Spirit that brings us joy.

It is the Spirit that is our wise counselor as we walk in the shadows.

It is the Spirit that is bright like a sun when we awaken.

In the double born the Spirit spreads and enlightens all areas of our hearts and minds.

It guides the Priests of the Sacred Way to the waters of life.

The double-born Priests have in their keeping all things worth the choosing.

These double-born Priests are guided in all things by love.

All mankind are capable of achieving this noble station.

# As a Faithful Servant

As a faithful servant of the One I call upon you.

I call upon you to accept the many gifts of the One.

In keeping with the love of the One I will share the knowledge and wisdom I have received.

As a faithful servant of the One I will share my words even with the indolent, the godless man.

I will share my words with the poor and the wealthy who have never brought an offering to the One.

In this way none may say they have not had the opportunity to know the teachings of the One.

The Mighty One is most splendid.

He gives all of humanity the opportunity to know the truth.

None are forced to change their foolish ways.

None are given more than they are ready to handle.

May we be among the first of our generation to walk in the Way of the One.

May we be true worshipers of the One.

# Heaven and Earth Have Trembled

Heaven and Earth have trembled at the might and voice of the One, The Holy One.
The Holy One has loved and helped all of mankind.
The unwise have resisted with all their might, His power and His teachings.
The wise have sought the friendship of the One by learning all they might of His Sacred Way.

The wise have sought to partake of His waters of life.

The wise, like true friends, will seek to do the work given to them by the One.
They will be prompt servants in making proper use of the Spirit they are given.
Great mental power is given to those who walk consistently in the Sacred Way.
Hearken to their words and songs.
They are the strong ones of the Master of the house.

The folk of ancient times glorified and honored the strong ones of the noble double birth.

They had the Mighty One as the power behind their words.
Today we too may become ones of the noble-double birth.
We may bring our love to the One and perform the Sacred Rite.
We may enjoy the strength that many think has been lost.

The people will prosper when they come to the One with their love.
They will become Righteous Ones who proclaim aloud the Holy Law.
Their power will come from the One, the Father of all mankind.
He will bind their work with His love.

On this great earth the One has sent His treasures to all who would walk in His Sacred Way.

Unstained by dust are His teachings to those who follow the Sacred Way. Within their neighborhoods the righteous will pray day and night to the One to guide their footsteps on the Way.

The flames of the Holy Spirit encircle those who serve in the Sacred Way. Of our own free will we serve the One. We are the sole determiners of whom or what we choose to serve. The Holy Spirit comes to those who freely give of their love.

To the Worshipers, Sages, and Priests who freely worship in love, the One sends His Holy Spirit.

The One will fulfill the desire of those who bring Him their love. To the One draw near, and endeavor to walk in the Sacred Way. The Spirit will come to you and be inclined to hear your words, prayer, and song.

As you begin to walk in the Sacred Way, you will be fed with milk. At first the direction you receive will be as if it was through the stirrings of your own mind.

As you continue as a Righteous One, deeper stirrings will guide you. The earnest soul will come to know the collective workings of the Spirit within and around them.

Rich strength of life is yours as you continue in the Sacred Way. The One will grant to you surpassing powers and far-extending might. Few indeed have been those who have reached the Godhead and the full bestowal of His Wealth of Knowledge and Wisdom.

# The Robe of the Holy Spirit

The robe of the Holy Spirit, which you put on, abounds with wondrous gifts.
Uninterrupted counsels are yours as you go about your daily tasks.
All falsehoods you will overcome as you closely hold to the eternal Law.

The might you receive, no one will be able to comprehend.
Truth is the crushing word, which you, as a Sage, will utter.
Those who hate the One God will run away and perish from your site.

The Holy Spirit existed before the creation of any creature.
This was established by the One, for the Spirit is His active power.
It is this Spirit that supports this entire world.
The Spirit fulfills the Law and overcomes all falsehood.

Those who take upon themselves the robe of the Spirit are always advancing.
Never will they be allowed to fall downward.
Wearing the robe of the Spirit you become inseparable from the One who gives you delight.

You become unbridled from limiting thoughts.
You maintain a youthful love of the mystery of the One.
The One will continue to surpass your Highest Thought.

The One will prosper in this world those who love Him and give to Him their full devotion.

May those who lead us be well skilled in the Sacred Rites.
May they call to the One to give us assistance and deepen our knowledge.

We will love and worship the One God.
Let us live in a way that will be a delight to Him.
May He favor us with His Love.

# We Worship the One

We worship the One with our reverence and love.

With our words, our thoughts, and our deeds we show our love.

When we praise the One we activate a mighty power.

We activate an impulse of loving energy within.

When we worship we receive immediate blessings.

The Spirit of the One within and around us is activated when we worship with love.

In our assemblies the One moves and presents us with gifts.

Better than a human priest the One shares with us His love.

The One bestows the waters of life upon His worshipers.

The One brings joy to our families and friends.

The ancient house-Lord gives us wisdom and knowledge when we give to Him our love.

# I Will Declare

I will declare the mighty deeds of the One God.
It is He who measured out all the regions of the earth.
It is He who measured out all the regions of the heavens.
It is He who receives the highest honor from the congregation.
It is He who has set down His footsteps for all religions to follow.

The One is found in all regions.
Within Him all living creatures have their habitation.
Without Him there would be no life.

The One is found in our common dwelling places.
The One is found in the far-ranging mountains.
The One is found within our hearts and minds.
The One is found in our churches and temples.
The One may be found wherever we may be.

With the One all places are filled with imperishable sweetness.
It would be a joy to list them, but there is not room.
Let it be said, the One upholds the earth, the heavens, and all living creatures.

May I attain to His standards.
May I be one of His well-loved.
May I reside with Him in my dwelling.
May I be one of the devoted, who are happy.
May I be allowed to partake of the waters of life.
May I be guided to follow in the footsteps of the Holy Way.

It is my greatest prayer that we may live in harmony and peace.
May the One always be with us in our dwelling place.
May I be found worthy to be called a Child of the One.

# The Children of the One

The Children of the One have an awesome task.
Their minds are set upon service to the One and mankind.
They are given to drink the waters of life.
On them is bestowed the Holy Spirit.
They are the twice born of the One.

The One God is never beguiled or fooled
The Children must live in accord with their noble birth.

To those who have accepted the Holy Spirit of the One, God comes.
He comes with all His might, knowledge, and wisdom.
They are directed well, these mortal men and women.
They in turn are to direct and guide mankind with love.
They may never turn aside from their noble birth.

They give their love to God and to mankind.
In return they are increased in mighty manly strength.
They bring, as it were, both parents to the attention of mortal mankind.

They take their place as a third or some may say a fourth in the heavens as a
light to all mankind.

To all they contact they bring the name of the Father's highest name.

To all they will speak of the Mighty One, the Father.
They will speak of the One who is the preserver of mankind.
They will speak of His bountiful gifts.
They will speak of His all-encompassing love.
They will speak of the freedom He gives to mankind.
They will speak of the purposes of life.

A mortal man will look with amazement on the twice born.
They will look with amazement on the light of knowledge of the twice born.
They will become restless with wonder at their deeds.
They may be tempted to look upon the twice born as gods.

None of the twice born will approach mankind as gods.
None dare compare themselves to the Mighty One.
All they do, they do to bring awareness to the people of the One.
They do all for the glory of the One.

Life on earth is like a rounded wheel.
It has been set in swift motion by the One.
Life has developed in a vast number of forms.
The One is with all who bring forth their praise.
The One comes to all at their call.

# The Children of God

The Children of God, as they go on their way, are to be helpful to all who need their aid.

They are to shine forth with the Spirit, which they have within.
They are god-like to mortal man.

The wise will share their love and praise of the One.
They will walk carefully striving to stay in the Sacred Way.
In all they do, they will demonstrate their love of the One.

The Children of God will bring all their love to the One who is the Ancient, the First, and the Last.

It is the One who, with His spouse, the Earth, has created the inhabitants of the earth.

Those who can tell of their lofty birth shall surpass in glory even their peers.

The One is He whom we strive to satisfy.
He places within us the primeval germ of Order.
From our birth we are aware of Him.

We know His name and have told all who would listen.
May we enjoy the grace of the Mighty One.

We wait to know the will of the One God.
It is He who guides our words and our deeds.
He is the power Supreme.
May we always be counted among His Friends.

Even the most high of the children has need of fellowship.
They need the fellowship of the One.
They need fellowship with their fellow man.

The One knows of our need.
He comes to help and guide His children.
They, in turn, come to help and guide mortal man.
All may share in fellowship with the One.
The One gives to the worshiper a share of Holy Law.
The One gives to all worshipers a share of His love.

# The Child of God

The Child of God is awakened.
They rise from the earth and from the cave of ignorance.
The mighty Spirit has placed upon them her light.

The child is equipped by the Spirit to walk the Holy course.
The One God has moved His children many different ways.

When the Spirit comes, our great power is knowledge and wisdom.
We are well equipped for all we might be assigned to do.
The One God will guide and strengthen us for each task.
We are given great delight by doing service for the One and in serving our
fellow man.

We are nourished by the Holy Spirit.
We are given to drink from the waters of life.
The days of our life are prolonged.
Our former trespasses of the law are wiped away.
Any foes we encounter are driven away.
The One is our companion and our friend.

The germ of eternal life is within all creatures.
It is within all living beings.
It has been given to all so that it might develop as we awaken.
Do not pass by this mighty power, which is hidden within all men and women.
Commit now to the Sacred Way, and be awakened from the slumber of a
foolish life.

Whatever skills we think now that we possess are nothing compared to those
we receive when we awaken.

Bring your love to the One.
Give Him your heart.
You will become one of the pure.
The One will pour out His gifts to you.

# Go to the One

Go to the One if you are willing.
Go to Him and receive His full counsel.
He will make you strong when you stand at His side.

Do not crave the wealth given to others.
You have great helpers waiting to aid you when you come to the One with a loving heart and mind.

Do not be concerned with what others may give you.
You have no need to seek their favor.
When you go to the One in loving worship He will give you gifts beyond compare.

He will awaken in you a deep understanding.
He will search your heart and fulfill your deepest longing.
Nothing can compare to receiving His loving care.

Take your seat as a child of the One.
You will be equipped for a great journey.
You will be given shelter and protection wherever you may go.
You will be guided in every step of the way.
Never again will you find that you are alone.

May these words help to awaken and preserve you.
May you commit to the Sacred Way.
May you receive the Spirit, which none can exhaust.
May you be guided to overcome all the obstacles you think are in your way.
Before you is the firm ground on which you may stand.

Many think they are securely bound by the material things of life.
Many think they are securely bound by situations or by caste.

Many think they will be devoured if they change their way.
Nothing binds you or devours you except you own heart and mind.

If you commit your heart and mind to the One you will find you are unbound in every way.

The One will aid you to reach your aim and end.
Whatever you may do; wherever you may go; The One will be your guide and friend.

# I Will Walk

I will walk in the Sacred Way.
I will honor the Spirit and the Earth.
I will honor these great strengtheners of law.
Honoring the Spirit and the Earth I am conjoined with the One, the Father of All.
Through His wonder-working wisdom choice boons are brought forth.

I will meditate upon the gracious Father's mind.
I will meditate upon the Mother's great inherent power.

These prolific parents have made the work of life.
For their children they have made all-'round immortality.

These parents have provided well for all their children.
They have given to them the skills to work.
They have given to the many wondrous powers.
They have brought forth life with all its wonders.

To keep the truth of all that stands and all that moves,
They guard the station of their children who know no guile.

Being most wise and having surpassing skill,
They have measured out a place for their children.
They have united together in their birth and their home.

Our parents are ever at hand to guide and protect their children.
They keep forever new the web of our existence.

This is today the goodliest gift of our Savior:
The thought we have now that the God is furthering us and protecting us.
On us He looks with loving-kindness.
Through His Spirit and the Earth He bestows upon us riches, wealth, and treasure.

# These Two

These two, the Spirit and the Earth, bestow prosperity on all.
They are the sustainers of the region.
They are inseparable from the Holy One who is exceedingly wise.
These two are used by the One God by fixed decree.

This wide-ranging pair never fail.
They are the Father and the Mother of all existing life.
They keep all creatures safe who learn and honor their power.

They are the two world-halves, the Spirited and the beautiful, because the
Father has clothed them in goodly forms.

The Sons and Daughters of these parents have a multitude of tasks.
Those who become the Priests have within them the power to cleanse our
hearts and minds.

Those who become the Sages sanctify the worlds with their surpassing
power.
Those who become the Teachers feed mankind the milk of knowledge till we
are ready for deeper wisdom.

Each day is spent preparing mankind for the deeper wisdom.

Most skilled is the One God.
It is He who made the two world-halves, which bring prosperity and life to all.
It is He who with great wisdom measured the regions out.
It is He who established them as pillars that shall never decay.

Extol in your worship and your songs, the Spirit and the Earth.
Extol the One who bestowed on us this mighty pair.
Contemplate His great glory and High Lordly sway.

Contemplate our place as His Children.
Contemplate how we may extend ourselves as guides to those who have not yet awakened.

May the One send us the strength and knowledge to accomplish this task.
May we do all for the glory of the One.

Printed in the United States
79055LV00004B/69